ONE MAN'S HEAVEN

EUGENE JACOBSON

*

WINGSPAN PRESS

Copyright © 2007 Eugene Jacobson
All rights reserved.

No part of this book may be used or reproduced in any manner without written permission of the author, except for brief quotations used in reviews and critiques.

This book is a work of fiction. Names, characters, settings and incidents are either the product of the author's imagination or used fictitiously. Any resemblance to actual events, settings or persons, living or dead, is entirely coincidental.

Printed in the United States of America

Published by WingSpan Press, Livermore, CA
www.wingspanpress.com

The WingSpan name, logo and colophon are the trademarks of WingSpan Publishing.

ISBN 978-1-59594-143-5

First edition 2007

Library of Congress Control Number 2007930005

Photo of Eugene Jacobson courtesy of David Jacobson..

Cover photo courtesy of Terry Sutherland.

Introduction and Acknowledgments

In the last year of his life, my father wrote this book. If he suspected he had cancer while he was writing, he never told us. By the time his diagnosis came in September 2006, he had finished his second draft. But because the book is Dad's personal vision of Heaven, I can't help but wonder whether he was, in effect, going ahead to prepare a room for himself.

Because Dad wasn't with us long enough to review this final version, I've edited only lightly, preserving his voice in all its Midwestern honesty, tenderness and vulnerability. His generosity also shines through—in his Heaven, even Hitler and Stalin have been forgiven, much to their astonishment. In working with my father's words, I often found myself astonished as well by the beauty and lyricism of certain passages. Other aspects were less surprising, such as his idiosyncratic references to northern pike, Cave People sex, and Republicans (who, like Hitler and Stalin, are also forgiven).

My father would want me to thank everyone who helped make this book possible, from his own family and friends to the ministers and theologians who influenced his thinking. I would like to thank my mother, Maxine Jacobson, for typing my father's work, an assignment she carried out all her married life. Many thanks, also, to Margee Gaeddert, who first edited the book and provided the illustrations, and to Ramone Munoz, who designed the cover.

As sincere as it is, this book only begins to unveil the man my father was. But I hope readers will enjoy this glimpse into his expansive soul and appreciate the openness of his vision of the Hereafter.

Tom Jacobson
February 2007

Chapter 1

In the Beginning
(OR "How I Got There")

Strange things happen in Oklahoma. For me, it was the strangest. Not the accident itself—that was pretty much Standard Operating Procedure.

I was tooling along about 70–only a little over the legal limit on Oklahoma City's Hefner Parkway. I was passed regularly in the light afternoon traffic headed south, toward downtown. A million-dollar-a-mile safety fence in the grassy area between the three lanes of traffic going north and south on each side. The fence gave me a feeling of security, sort of. Only three feet high, the protective cable fence had worked very well in its first year, lowering crossover fatalities to *almost* none. However, I learned that like all cure-alls, the fence didn't always work. I could see what was going to happen. A semi began to pass a car in the middle lane of the northbound traffic, over-corrected when he pulled out to pass, lost control, headed diagonally into the million-dollar fence and aimed (allowing for our speeds in opposite directions) toward my side of the parkway, the fence–and me! Would the fence hold, at least deflecting the semi less directly into my path? Maybe even back to its own side of the freeway? It didn't.

I had already slowed down to a little over 50 in the few

seconds that had gone by. Then I had to decide–should I speed up and hope to get past the space the truck would soon occupy on my side of the road? Or should I hit the brakes, ease left, trying to hit the rear of the truck with a glancing blow that would send me toward the expensive fence, which would stop me, not fatally (perhaps). Nope–too late to speed up–just hit the brakes, guide my car to the left. It wasn't going to work. I would die in the crash. "Oh, God–help me!" Then, the sound of crushing metal and smashing glass building to a roar. Neat, no sounds. Just darkness. Not even a light at the end of a tunnel. Nothing.

I woke up lying on a *very* comfortable bed. In fact, the most comfortable that I could ever remember. I seemed to be outdoors but was lightly shaded by a filmy awning. Air circulated gently through the open sides of a tent-like framework that surrounded me. The light was unusually soothing–dim enough to be restful to my eyes but clear enough for me to make out two vague figures talking together in a far corner of the tent. The shorter man, clean-shaven, a little over six feet tall, gestured rather wildly and talked loudly. The taller, more muscular, bearded man, handsomely robed, remained calm and composed. They both spoke in English! Although I couldn't make sense out of the few words I heard.

I was pretty sure that I was dead. Certainly I was no longer on Earth. But was this Heaven or Hell? Or was it just a Waiting Place between Earth and Eternity? I felt no pain. My shirt and pants weren't even wrinkled. The two figures began to approach me. The basketball player-sized man had a large decorative P monogrammed on his whiter-than-white robe. He must be St. Peter! Wow! His deep, friendly voice rumbled at me. "Welcome to Heaven. Yes, I am St. Peter. We have arranged time so that if Newcomers expect to see me when they enter Heaven, I will be there. This is your personal Heavenly Guide, Roger. He will stay with you as long as you need him for information and support." Then St. Peter was gone.

Still in shock about St. Peter, I asked Roger, "Does St. Peter greet *everyone* who gets to Heaven? Are there so few Newcomers?"

"Yes, he does greet everyone, usually Christians who expect to see him here. Sometimes, as in your case, he greets individuals, sometimes groups. And, no, there are not just a few Newcomers each day. Many, many people die each day–and come directly to Heaven. With the Chinese population as large as it is, even with their birth controls, we have an enormous number of Asians who arrive here daily. Because, yes, everyone does make it to Heaven! But St. Peter just greets Christians, who know about him."

"Oh, so all people do go to Heaven?

"Yes, there is Universal Salvation. For people of all religions, all races, even those who can't quite believe in God or Heaven."

"My wife, Maxine, believes strongly in Universal Salvation, although it's not very popular on Earth."

"Yes, some of the regular-church-going, tithing, rule-minded folks are a little surprised, even *upset,* when they first arrive in Heaven, to find that God's Grace includes all sinners, all of the Newcomers from Earth. But the stiffnecks soon get over their surprise and being upset. The Joy of Heaven overwhelms them, so they truly begin to worship God and help their fellow Earthlings. That's what Heaven's all about!"

"I can hardly wait to have you show me around Heaven. I already have lots of questions!"

"Yes, we know. But you need to remember that you are no longer a college professor. You're no longer in charge. You will listen and be quiet. (You'll notice that I didn't say, 'Shut up!' In your family, you and your sons were properly conditioned to avoid using those harsh words. Thank God!)"

"O.K., but is it all right if I ask questions if anything's not clear?"

"Certainly. But try to control yourself. You're in Heaven now. Understanding and remembering are easier here. Everything that I say to you is received and recorded in your brain, like a computer back on Earth. We've borrowed a good deal of the good computer theory from Earth, without getting all tied up in the hardware and programs. God the Father gets quite a kick out of developing His own new programs which are especially tuned to the needs of Heaven. From now on, you'll never forget anything of value that you see, hear, touch, smell or taste in Heaven. And don't give me any grief about my use of *never* and *always* and other similar words as bad generalizations which are not true. If I use those words they will be true here in Heaven, you know for sure."

"Sorry, Roger. (May I be that informal?) You're reading my thoughts already."

"Yes, you may be informal with me. And I'll just call you Jake. I have been reading your thoughts, Jake, ever since we first met. God and all Heavenly staff members (including me) have special equipment so that we can read the thoughts of any Earth person within 100 feet. Even picking out the individual we're interested in."

"Sounds pretty complicated to me."

"God loves to solve any hang-ups in Heaven, so He puts in new computer equipment and programs all the time. If a Fact, an Opinion, your Reaction to an unusually beautiful sunset is in your head, I can snap it up quickly, without you even knowing it."

"Sounds a little scary, but this is Heaven, so I guess I'll just relax. What you learn won't be used to get me in trouble or sent to Hell."

"Correct. Ah–one other thing–make your questions and comments as brief as possible. Not only do you need to work on your Earthly sin of talking too much, usually too loudly (my Heavenly hearing is very good) but also the sin of too many details."

"The Joy of Heaven already overwhelms me. I can accept your suggestions gladly. Yes, my talking too much got me in trouble with friends (and unfriendlies), causing me more than a little fuss and bother. (Although calling such behavior a sin seems a little strong to me.)"

"So you learned from your major mistake on Earth? You changed? Talked less?"

"Unfortunately for me (and them, I suppose), I didn't. Their criticism bothered me, but I convinced myself they were wrong. Here in Heaven, your comments seem to be only friendly persuasion. But I—"

One Man's Heaven

Roger held up a hand for me to stop. Grinning broadly and kindly, he tried to cool me down with, "Now, now! I understand. Just remember we have time to work on this—Eternity is such a good idea! And don't worry. You seem to be an excellent candidate for making necessary changes so you'll be a good 'fit' in Heaven."

"I don't have much choice in the matter, do I?"

"No, you don't. But God will help you to adapt yourself to Heaven. And it won't be painful. Another note about your personal growth in Heaven. When you told your collection of stories, jokes, etc. (especially in your classes) you remember the groans and occasional jeers you sometimes got from your listeners. In an effort to rid Heaven of some of those often-repeated gems with which you bored and bothered others, every time you tell one of these jewels, it will disappear from your mind, never to be recalled and repeated again, making room in your brain for new ideas and making Heaven better."

"Are my stories that bad?"

"I hope we'll never find out. Please don't feel that you're being singled out by this rule. All amateur jokers, story tellers, pithy sayers, and chatterboxes are treated equally in Heaven:'One and done!' The result: improved individuals and a more perfect Heaven."

"Suppose I catch myself in time? If I don't say it, I won't lose it?"

"Correct. But it's amazing how difficult it is for everyone not to blab, to hold it in."

"Oh, I feel a joke coming on! I've nearly worn it out, so I guess I'll tell you and then forget it, happily."

"Shoot."

As I told my joke, images appeared briefly on a mysterious TV screen hanging in the air, then faded into the background and disappeared.

"This is from my college days at St. Olaf in Minnesota, so after over 50 years, it's ready to leave me. A Lutheran named John died, went to Heaven, and was standing near the Pearly Gates with St. Peter. John looked down a hill toward a small lake where family members frolicked in the water and on the shore. 'Who are they, St. Peter?' They're Baptists.' 'And in that wooded area, with families sitting on blankets, eating chicken dinners from their picnic baskets? Who are they, St. Peter?' 'Those are the Methodists.' 'And why is that 15-foot brick wall over there, St. Peter?' 'That's for the Lutherans inside. They think they're the only ones to make it here.' Hmmm—I think I feel better after getting that out of my system."

"You should. I've heard of old chestnuts before, but I think that one had sprouted!" Roger grinned. The kidding tone in his voice suggested only a light-hearted, Heavenly ribbing. I smiled back. "What was it we were talking about? Some joke or other? Maybe now you could tell one?"

"No thanks. We've been trained as guides not to get into the joke-telling trap. Wastes too much time. By the way, my slightly heated discussion with St. Peter, when you first saw us?"

"Yes, at that time, you were not very clear figures. I noticed you waving your arms. What was that all about?"

"I was upset about being selected as your guide. I had just completed a rather long-term introduction to Heaven for a hard-headed Swede!"

"And knowing I was half-Swedish on my father's side, you thought that I would be another tough one?"

"At least I thought I deserved a break of some kind. But with St. Peter, while He doesn't mind hearing any objections a guide has, he seldom changes His mind. Once every couple of centuries is his usual rate. Actually, we tell time a little differently in Heaven, pretty hard to understand. Einstein took only about five minutes to figure it out. But you're no Einstein, so we'll leave it for later."

"Are you giving me a bad time? Is this what humor is like in Heaven–sarcastic?"

"No, you're right! I was kidding you. And all guides are trained to avoid humor. If I quit, does it mean you won't tell any more of your worn-out jokes?"

Now it was my turn to grin. "I make no such promises!" We were getting acquainted–and this guide seemed like a winner!

One Man's Heaven

"Forgive me, but I'd like to tell you a little about this Swede I once guided. Talking about him may help get him out of my head."

"Be my guest. I'm always eager to hear what others have to say about Swedes. Of course, I'm half Norwegian and half Swedish, so you can imagine how mixed up I am!"

"Guiding this Swede was slow work. He didn't change his mind easily or quickly. Several times he suggested to me that Heaven should change to fit in with his beliefs."

"Sounds like a pretty typical Swede to me. How did you finally handle him?"

"I suggested that he spend a few weeks in Hell. That's something that guides are seldom allowed to suggest. He ignored my suggestion, although I think he would have been happier in Hell than he was in Heaven at that time. I finally just wore him down. He took the first steps to beginning Eternity, at peace with God and Heaven."

"Good for you! With God to hold you up, you can even overcome a Swede."

"The main reason that I joined you was that St. Peter had listened to me calmly and quietly when I begged for a break. Then St. Peter he said: ' You can do this job well. It won't be as difficult as the last time. Nor will it continue as long. Just do it!' Then he disappeared."

"That's pretty clear. And you did it."

"When St. Peter is that definite, I not only accept his authority without further questions, I know that when he looks into the future, he can predict what will happen. You will be easier than the Swede–maybe even enjoyable at times."

"What better place for a positive attitude!"

"And, really, you've already turned out much better than I had hoped. Why, you even have a place in your heart for some Republicans!"

"Some of my best friends (even close relatives) are Republican. But I guess that if God wants us to pray for everyone, even our enemies, I should be able to pray for some Republicans. I hope that I make the necessary changes so that I can become an acceptable part of Heaven. Just so I don't have to play one of those [ ] harps!"

7

Eugene Jacobson

To my surprise, my rather strong adjective describing harps did not make any sound in the Heavenly air. Just a blank space, a word missing in my sentence. My shocked look made Roger laugh out loud.

"I'll spell out a few of the problem words that can't be heard in Heaven. In addition to da-m-n-e-d which you used, s-h-i-t and p-i-s-s are common omissions. The F word and the N word can't even be spelled out. We're changing though. For centuries, we weren't even allowed these forbidden words when spelled out. Of course, God and Jesus Christ, together with sacred words such as Yahweh from other Earthly religions, disappear into thin air when these words are used as curses or swearing. Such word problems are not frequent in Heaven. Soon after newcomers arrive in Heaven, they change, almost unconsciously, as they note the absence of these emotion-laden words. All vulgar words simply disappear. Perhaps we should recall the Old Testament rule 'Let your communication be yea, yea and nay, nay, for whatsoever is more than this cometh of evil.'"

"Does anybody have any trouble with this Heavenly law?"

"We've had a few Newcomers who chose to go to Hell so they could curse and rant and rave as they had on Earth. Most of them were back in Heaven in a day or two. You can choose to leave Hell at any time. Oath-addicted Mark Twain gave Hell a try. He only lasted a couple hours, however. For him Hell wasn't particularly interesting or creative. Hell only included (for him) the heat, cold, near-drowning, etc, that has been known as Hell since Dante's first imaginings of The Inferno."

"Whoa!" I raised my hand for Roger to stop talking.

"We'd better get on with the Ten Amendments, so we'll have a better organization of our questions and discussion."

"What Ten Amendments? What do you mean?"

Chapter 2

Another Perfect 10
(OR "How About This Heaven?")

I carried the double-spaced sheet over to a nearby oak tree, propped myself up against the trunk, and began to read. Roger just watched me.

Amendment #1: You feel great joy because you are in Heaven. (And it only gets better.)

Amendment #2: When you arrive in Heaven, your body will be the age and the weight that you were when you died. You may experiment with any changes that you wish to make. (Ask your guide for complete instructions.)

Amendment #3: At first, what you see and hear in Heaven will be what you expected Heaven to be. (This Heaven will change.)

Amendment #4: Not long after you get to Heaven, you will choose whether you wish to remain in Heaven, return to Earth, or go to Hell. (You may visit Hell at any time, returning to Heaven whenever you want. Few remain in Hell very long.)

Amendment #5: There is no sex in Heaven (neither in thought nor action). God tried permitting sex for the first people who came to Heaven, the Cave People. But it was just too noisy and created too many problems. God's decision for No Sex has been final for centuries and is not apt to be changed.

Amendment #6: You may visit the members of your family who got to Heaven before you did. (Special permission is required if you visit family members in Hell.) Do not expect too much of your first visit, especially if you are Lutheran. You will recognize one another easily, probably kiss and embrace (unless you are of Scandinavian descent). You will probably find that your family members have already made a smooth transition to Heaven and will feel much closer to God than to you.

Amendment #7: You will quickly learn that whatever you do in Heaven is a means of worshiping God–and serving your fellow Newcomers. No special churches or altars or rituals are used. But, yes, there are helpful Angels–most of them with harps–who will assist you if you have any questions or need advice about proper worship.

Amendment #8: Everyone goes to Heaven when they die. The idea of Universal Salvation is not accepted by all Newcomers when they first enter Heaven. We must remember: God makes the rules here. With all the varying Earthly ideas about Heaven which the Newcomers bring with them, at first there are many Heavens. God allows all Newcomers to find Heaven as they imagined it. Gradually, they learn to accept God's Heaven. And the real thing is much better!

Amendment #9: Feel free to try as many Heavenly experiences and activities as you like. Your goal is to decide how you will worship God and serve your neighbors in Heaven for Eternity. No rush: You may make changes in your plans at any time, with no limit on the number of changes that you make. With Eternity, you have plenty of time.

Amendment #10: Enjoy new learning for yourself, improved communication with other Heavenly residents, and especially your increased ability to love others, including God and the Angels, as well as Earthlings like yourself. At times you may even think you're right up there with God. (Don't worry, you're not!)

I quickly finished reading the last of the Ten Amendments, looked up, and Roger began our discussion.

Chapter 3

Great Joy in Heaven
(OR "Notice the Difference?")

Roger looked at me, smiled, and repeated Amendment # 1: "You feel great joy because you are in Heaven. (And it only gets better.)"

"You've noticed in our talking so far that I've made a few critical remarks about your Earthly beliefs and behavior. But you didn't feel any anger or even mild irritation. That's because everything I say is for your own good. You accept this in Heaven, while you had lots of trouble with criticism on Earth. You felt this true concern immediately when you arrived in Heaven. It's in the air and in your heart."

"No problem. I'm with you so far."

"Great! When I say *God*, I'm not going through the Holy Triumvirate of Father, Son, and Holy Spirit every time as I explain about how Heaven is set up, governed, and modified by the Big Three-in-One. I expect you, especially as a Christian and Lutheran, to do this in your head without prompting. God has made every effort to make all Newcomers happy, positive, and open to making changes rapidly in adapting to Heaven's Amendments."

"I feel free of sin, willing to do God's will rather than my own. I'm really enjoying my Heavenly home already!"

"It's easier for you than for many other Newcomers. Your

beliefs about Heaven and how it works were so vague that you don't have to get rid of many wrong ideas. Actually, you didn't believe in much!"

"Sorry. May we chat about some of the problems other Newcomers have when they get to Heaven? I have no objection to problems as long as they belong to someone else."

"I'm concerned about your Christian attitude toward the problems of others, but we'll work on that later. But any criticism, any gloating about how 'I am better than they are' is strictly forbidden. Your change of attitude makes Heaven better for you–and you are more suitable for Heaven. Incidentally, when a rare and unwanted criticism slips out of you, the Holy Spirit hiccups."

"Anything I do wrong in Heaven causes the Holy Spirit to hiccup? Unbelievable!"

"Believe it. The Holy Spirit reacts in this way to hate or even dislike in any form (thought, word, or deed). The Holy Spirit is extremely tender-hearted and uses this method to remind everyone in Heaven about love and charity . With hiccups, the Holy Spirit stops everything for 30 seconds in Heaven. No one can move or talk. The guilty sinner in Heaven is not identified, but all the Newcomers are super-careful about their thoughts and actions from then on. And the sound! A rasping, breathy hiccup that is soul-shaking! On average, the Holy Spirit has to hiccup only a time or two each century. It's an effective tool for improvement in Heaven."

"But why don't the other parts of the Holy Trinity take a vote on the Spirit hiccuping?"

"The Holy Trinity could operate that way, but It has chosen not to concern Itself with the infrequent, mild, and usually brief bouts of the Holy Spirit's hiccups. Exactly why, God alone knows."

"What particular things in Heaven upset God the Father and God the Son?"

Roger shook his head. "I don't know. Perhaps they will reveal more about themselves during Eternity. I know that God is upset by the wars, the hunger, and the other results of hatred on Earth. More than that, God knows."

"Okay. In the meantime, I'll try very hard not to make the Holy Spirit hiccup."

"And you'll do extremely well, because God will help you."

"Incidentally, what about those people who believe in the Rapture? What if they're snatched up into Heaven while they're driving? I've always worried about those driverless cars causing accidents."

"You're like the rest of us–what you worry about probably won't happen. Didn't you find in your life on Earth that the things you worried about the most often turned out differently than you expected? Thank God. And if it did happen, you learned to accept it, perhaps even to understand why."

"Give me an example of how that works, please."

"A woman prayed for a child in her marriage. Both she and her husband were over 30, no longer used birth control, graduate school was ending, and they hoped to have a baby soon."

"Sounds like a familiar story…"

"I thought it might. After seeing a number of doctors, they were told that it would be difficult for the woman to get pregnant. They were in the last year of residency for his graduate degree, with no money saved up, no teaching positions opening for him the following year—and the wife became pregnant! So there the main breadwinner was–still in school, no prospects for a job, and about to become a first-time father. The man had some strange symptoms after a couple weeks. Later in the day, his upper lip felt numb, followed often by the same feeling on his forehead. When he went to the doctor's office, the M. D. asked, 'Are you worried about something?' After his concerns were listed, the doctor just nodded his head and prescribed a mild tranquilizer until some of the problems were solved. Their first child, a boy, was born. The man got a job and stopped using the tranquilizer. The three of them crossed half the U. S. to begin the man's new teaching job. As the boy grew older, the wife began to worry about him. No big signs, but she began to wonder if their son might be gay. Her prayers went out to God: 'Don't let him be gay! Please, God.'"

"And God answered her prayers?"

Eugene Jacobson

"Yes, He did. Toward the end of his high school years the son told his parents that he was gay. They were mildly surprised but more concerned about what his life would be like. The mother renewed her prayers. Finally, she realized that God had answered her prayers."

"And the answer was...?"

"A change would be made in the son's life and in hers. She needed to accept him for what he was–a gay person. He was still a good student, a good son, and a good Christian. God had answered her prayers, but not with the answer that she expected."

"And God was right?"

"He was. Their son now has a very good job and is busy writing plays. Which keep getting better and better–not just in his parents' eyes but also, in the eyes of the critics. He is still gay, but his mother's attitude has changed. Her prayers were answered. God isn't as interested in our sex lives on Earth as we are. He is more concerned that we should love Him and all of our neighbors (all humans) on Earth and in Heaven. And we do hurt our neighbors when we treat them as things, not people. God is upset at this behavior, whether the misuse of others is in sex, working conditions, inadequate salaries, or hunger. On Earth, humans must concern themselves with the health and happiness of all humanity."

I think I got Roger's point. "Our concern for others begins in having the right attitude, which then leads to the right action."

Roger continued: "We need to get on with how God wants us to have more joy in our lives, not only in Heaven, but on Earth. It may seem to be too late for you to do anything for those still on Earth, but God may help you to reach people still living there."

"A strange hint of encouragement. I'm already dead. How can we have Heaven on Earth?"

"We can begin by simply following the guidelines that God has already given us in the Ten Commandments. Do you want the long explanation, such as Martin Luther's, or fairly brief answers to your questions about how the Ten Commandments can show us how we can have an Earth more like Heaven? Here goes Number One: 'You shall have no other gods before me.' If we could give up money, power, things (a big house, car, boat, etc.), even how we put our families in first place, instead of God, we'd be happier on Earth. These other gods would not distract us from our primary goal: knowing and loving God. We would learn to 'fear, love, and trust God above all other things.' This would give us an unshakeable foundation for our God-centered life on Earth."

"Briefly?"

"Okay, Number Two: 'You shall not take the name of the Lord your God in vain.' This seems to be a tough one for most Americans. From the little old lady in church who says, 'My God, it's hot today!' or to the variations of 'My God' on television, we let God's name slip off our tongues too easily in surprise, anger, even lying. We need to save God's name for prayer, giving thanks, and offering a comforting word to others."

Roger continued, "And Number Three: 'Remember the Sabbath Day to keep it holy.' This means that, yes, believers should meet together at least once a week. For instance, Muslims pray together five times a day. We need to learn more about God's wishes for us on Earth, both by reading the Scriptures and through talking to God in prayer. We need to be reassured that God is with us on Earth."

"No question about that!"

"And on to the Fourth Commandment: 'Honor your father and mother, that it may be well with you, and you may live long on the Earth.' We learn how to work with and value other people. We show respect for and follow the good rules of our parents. As we grow older, we, like the Prodigal Son, may make mistakes in our lives. But our parents forgive us and still love us. And God is the best Father to all of us. He is unchanging in His love and concern. This knowledge helps us experience Heaven on Earth."

Roger went on without a pause, "And the Fifth Commandment: 'You shall not kill. Not only must we avoid injury (physical or psychological) to the people in our everyday lives, but we must help them in any way we can. A cheerful greeting, a compliment, even just a smile will be a small way to help others get a taste of the Joy of Heaven on Earth!"

"What about the literal killing which society accepts? Capital punishment and abortion, for instance."

"The Roman Catholic Church is consistent on both counts–no abortions or capital punishment. Many Catholics in various parts of the world do not support their church–they practice abortion and agree on their government's use of capital punishment. And the United States not only makes abortion legal but, unlike most progressive Western countries, such as England, France, Germany, and the Scandinavian countries, still uses capital punishment as a threat to those who commit homicide. Although this threat does not seem very successful in lowering the number of murders in the U.S. And yet, there is the hope for eliminating capital punishment. Look how long it took the United States to get rid of slavery (and its connected problems later). Or even to allow women to vote. Progress is being made in the U.S. and throughout the Earth. But in the meantime, too many of the poor are in a Hell on Earth because we do not meet their needs. We can change life on Earth just as God changes us in Heaven. We'd better get back to the Ten Commandments."

"We've been preaching to ourselves. Do you think that we can sneak this message back to some of the folks on Earth?" I wondered.

"Not unless God would help you."

"But God doesn't work that way."

"Isn't that up to Him, not you? Maybe God will find a way for our discussion to get back to Earth."

"I hope! Are we up to Number Six? Already?"

"No sarcasm. Yes, we need to talk about the Sixth Commandment: 'You shall not commit adultery.'"

"A lot of people in the world have trouble with this one."

"In the United States about 50% of the marriages end in divorce. In your home state of Oklahoma, the divorce rate is rising toward 75%! Evidently, sex as the basis of marriage (as it is in most marriages) is a matter of temporary faithfulness to a partner. Sometimes for a relatively brief period. If marriage is mostly for the sake of having children, this goal, too, seems too weak for many humans. But the problems of adultery: anger, lying, money lost due to a divorce—apart from the basic ethical questions—make for more Hells on Earth than almost any other problem in modern life."

"What about those who live together but are not married?"

"God isn't as concerned about marriage as many people on Earth are. He realizes that a public ceremony in a church does not solve the many problems of people living together, married or not. People need to care about their partners, love them, and forgive them for all their mistakes. Perhaps one of the most serious errors that we make on Earth is to be angered by the problems of illness, business, and even daily living. We have not learned to differentiate between the little things, like not putting the cap on the toothpaste or hanging up clothes, to major conflicts about politics, even religion. God wants us to know that we should expect the sad, the frightening as part of life. But we need to remember that we are to call on Him for help and love when the world is too much for us. We'll always get an answer when we ask, although it will not always be the answer we wanted or expected."

"Is that why God eliminated sex from Heaven, because it was too complicated for Him—and for the Joy and Peace of Heaven? Or the Cave People were just too noisy?"

"Yes, they were, and evidently the noise just kept getting worse. On Earth, sex can cause much lying, plus physical and psychological abuse. God couldn't even straighten that out in Heaven."

"I probably shouldn't even ask this, but do some folks choose Hell to make up for the lack of sex in Heaven?"

"Yes, mostly guys, but a fair number of women, too. However it's as the Vietnam veteran commented (he was undoubtedly preceded by a Greek, or even an Egyptian, soldier) 'I don't know of anything else that I get behind on faster -- or caught up on sooner!' Like most visitors to Hell, the sex seekers are usually back in Heaven in a couple days."

"I believe it!"

"Going on. Commandment Number Seven: 'You shall not steal.' Most people on Earth don't steal money or property directly. But in capitalism, trashy products are sold for more than they are worth. Or a salesperson sells customers products or services which they do not need or charges too much. The excuse is: 'Everybody does it!' or 'I've got to make a living.' Many people are made unhappy, and, usually, even the sellers are not proud about what they've done. All of us need to deal fairly and honestly with each other. We will feel better, happier, more loved. Earth will be more like Heaven."

"Hey, we're moving along! What about the Eighth Commandment: 'You shall not bear false witness against your neighbor.' Luther wrote that we should 'defend him, speak well of him, and put the best construction on everything he does.' That's about the only part of Luther's explanation of the Ten Commandments that I remember."

"And you know why?"

"Yep—I tend to believe the worst details of the gossip I hear. I can spot the lies in political gossip easily, such as the wild story that President Clinton had a man murdered during his presidential campaign. I can easily believe that people will lie to win elections. Only the people who hated Clinton to begin with believed that one. We believe the gossip which agrees with the ideas we already have. Also, if we hear about someone in our church who has been unfaithful to his wife, we accept the story only too willingly. We feel superior, not having done that, rather than trying to understand, to help, to be charitable. I need to admit my feelings of superiority and prejudice and, at the very least, not repeat the gossip I've heard. Even nowadays we may hear someone, often white-haired, saying that all Catholics (or Baptists, Missouri Synod Lutherans, Mormons, or some other religion) tell us that we will never make it to Heaven."

"Certainly years ago such statements were often made. But now, thanks be to God, we no longer believe that we're better than other believers (and agnostics), who believe differently than we do. We should at least question the speaker of such gossip."

One Man's Heaven

Roger continued: "Folks forget that if they automatically believe the worst about someone or some group, this belief will color their whole outlook on life. The more negative people are, the more unhappy they'll probably be—not only about others, but also themselves. We can't be Pollyannas either. All is not right in the world. We need to speak up. We should be opposed to injustices of any kind, such as disliking someone because of color or religious beliefs—simply because they're different from us. To look for the good, not the weaknesses in others. To be more than ready to forgive others, and ourselves more completely. We need to avoid repeating the negative stories about others. We'll be happier and life on Earth will be better. That's how God wants to reward us with this commandment."

"What about guys like Hitler and Stalin? Surely, they're in Hell."

"No, they're here in Heaven. Do you think God's love and grace have the same human limits that you have?"

"That's outrageous! If those two killers are here in Heaven, I'm not sure I want to be here!"

"You're not the first person to say this, of course. But think a little: are you more intelligent, more loving, more powerful than God Himself?"

"What did Hitler and Stalin think about finding themselves in Heaven?"

"They couldn't believe it. They insisted on being sent to Hell. As I told you earlier, all of our Newcomers are offered a choice when they get here. But their trips to Hell don't work out—Hell is too loud, too hateful, too bloody. God treats those who go to Hell as He treats all of the Newcomers in Heaven. This means that each person sees Hell as he imagined it would be. It was too gory, even for Hitler and Stalin. Hitler went back to Heaven fairly quickly. Stalin took quite a bit longer, but he finally chose Heaven, too. They both shuffled back and forth between Heaven and Hell a few more times. It became a running joke in Heaven: 'Are they both in Heaven with us? Or are they both in Hell?' They were almost yoyos. They often met coming and going. At first they just nodded as they passed, but eventually they stood up, bowed to one another, and shouted a greeting as their Heavenly Carpets flew in opposite directions. They never could get the hang of just thinking themselves into either Heaven or Hell. They were in the nearly 2% of our Newcomers who never did figure it out. They were allowed to stay. Heaven makes compromises, too. They're both in Heaven now, permanently."

"Do they have anything to do with one another? Does anyone else associate with them?"

"Oh, yes. Actually, they're rather popular here in Heaven. Albert Einstein and Sigmund Freud play poker with them quite often. Hitler and Stalin are better poker players. For them, poker faces come easily."

"Do they use regular poker chips? What are the chips worth? You don't have to buy anything in Heaven, do you?"

"No, you don't have to buy anything in Heaven. If you need something, you just think of it, and—poof!—it's in front of you. But God the Father has a little joke with the poker chips. The chips are made of old gold halos that the Angels have worn out over the centuries. The Angels keep taking the halos off and putting them on the invisible halo holders, as they work. The removal and replacement wears the halos down. Because Angel halos are rather large and heavy, I think God was experimenting with halos at an earlier time. The modern halos were first made about the time the King James translation of the Bible was published, about 1603. These modern halos are lighter and more easily worn. But the Angels preferred the old heavier halos. God didn't care, but the worn-out halos were beginning to pile up, so God the Father decided to reuse them as poker chips. They're very bright and shiny—and extremely heavy. The poker players don't seem to mind the weight but are careful not to drop them on their sandal-covered feet. The $100 chips show Hitler on the front side and a tank on the back; for the $500 chip, Stalin is on the front, a plane on the back; the $1000 chip has Freud on the front and a couch on the back; the $5000 chip has Einstein on the front and $E=MC^2$ on the back."

"Wow! Those chips must be pretty valuable—collector's items!"

"No, anytime anyone wants to play poker, the chips are free. Players each get a little black notebook in which a record is kept of their gains and losses."

"But aren't players like Einstein and Freud big losers if Hitler and Stalin usually win?"

"Ah, but we're in Heaven. God is in charge. Over time, regardless of how much each player has lost or won, the balance for each player stays amazingly close to about $10,000. Some players have figured out that God has a hand in all this, but they just smile and keep on raising their bids."

"So, who wins?"

"No one. Everyone. Players may win or lose in an individual game, but, overall, everyone comes out even. This is Heaven—everyone who wants to gets to play; nobody loses. Incidentally, none of the Holy Trinity wears a halo. Instead, each is surrounded by a bubble of light whenever He travels around Heaven. When They appear together occasionally (only about once or twice a century in Earth time—for a special Harp Concert of both Angels and Newcomers, for example), the Three of Them together produce a dazzling light that none of us can look at directly."

"And when will I get to see such a display and hear such a concert?"

"As I said, in a century or so."

"I'll try to be patient. And we were talking about...?"

"Ah, yes. I'm a bit like many of our modern pastors and priests who would rather talk about theology than practical religion."

"Number Nine, Number Nine..."

"Commandment Number Nine: 'You shall not covet your neighbor's house.' Perhaps this is too narrow, but we are told not to do anything which would cause our neighbor to lose his house, his home. Many of us have seen large, richly furnished homes that make our homes seem modest, even shabby. Nothing should cause us to wish for anything bad to happen to our neighbor and his house. God rewards us because God is there with us, where we live with joy and love. God makes our lives easier, better."

"Good. I don't understand your explanation completely, but you helped me to see the *do* instead of just the *don't* in the Commandments. Commandment Ten is similar: 'You shall not covet your neighbor's wife nor his manservant ...his maidservant ...his cattle nor any thing that is your neighbor's.'"

"Pretty sound advice. If we put God first, and then, as the Tenth Commandment reminds us, we make our neighbor's happiness our greatest desire, and we will have the beginning of our own Heaven on Earth. The message from God is 'Make Me first, most important in your life, then you won't be tempted to possess your neighbor's wife or any of what he owns.' No sweat? Maybe. Your honest work (physical and mental) will make you earn what you have in life. Again, you'll enjoy Heaven while still on Earth!"

"That does it? Try to use the positive side of the Ten Commandments?"

"Correct. Turn *not* into *I will*—then you'll recognize God's blessings on Earth now, and not have to wait for the Joys of Heaven. But, when you get there, Heaven will still be even better than you hope."

"Whatever happened to 'Brevity is the soul of wit?' It seems we've forgotten."

"We'll do better on the next Amendment."

Chapter 4

Your Body in Heaven
(OR "Lord, Please Help Me!")

"I'll believe your bragging about brief when I hear it!"
"Ah, ye of little...hope! But I hope—much understanding."
"Go for it!"
"Amendment Two, as it appears on the hard copy: 'When you arrive in Heaven, your body will be the age and weight you were when you died. You may experiment with any body changes that you wish to make. (Ask your Guide for complete instructions.)' Do you need a little time to think about this or are you ready to ask me right now?"
"Please tell me what people usually do. How long do these changes take? How many times may I change?"
"The number of your changes is unlimited. Most people wait until after we discuss this Amendment, which may take only a few hours or up to several days. I believe Einstein holds the record for asking about the Second Amendment: 5 months, 5 days, and 5 hours. He asked a lot of questions. Wore out ten Guides and had the last Guide blubbering a couple times before the discussion ended."
"What was God's reaction? Was He upset?"
"No, He knew that Einstein was a special case, and just left it to St. Peter. As everybody works in Heaven, we only have ourselves to blame if the Work takes longer than

expected. Einstein was a professor, so that's why you heard me protesting to St. Peter when you woke up in Heaven. I remembered Einstein; I think I was Guide #3. And I'm a very poor blubberer! St. Peter assured me that you'd be much easier than Einstein. He's a lot smarter than you are, so he asked more good questions than you will."

"Thanks a lot—no, you're probably right. Please continue."

"And with your comment about being *brief*, I have new hope."

"Yes, but I want to experience Heaven more, not just talk about it."

"Wait, to answer your question—*briefly*—People tend to choose a younger age, especially if they're in the Older Group, as you are."

"I'm only 78! (Just giving you a hard time.) I've been through the Golden Years and similar hooey, so I'm only too willing to be called an Earth Oldster."

"Folks usually want to be younger, so their parents, other relatives and friends who died years before will still recognize them. No need to worry--God the Father has all that worked out. Regardless of which age you choose, the other person will see you as they remember you, due to God's special plan. Your father may see you as a teenager, while at the same time your Mother will see you as a 30 year-old with two children. Two different images of you at the same time."

"Seems like a lot of bother for God to go to! Couldn't He do something simpler?"

"God the Father enjoys making these special adjustments in Heaven. Most people choose the age they were when they died, although often with fewer wrinkles, less fat. And—the men particularly—more hair."

"So we can look as good as we want to? In my case, a smaller nose, more muscles, trimmer?"

"Yes, and those people who don't know you will see you exactly the way you changed to, unlike your family and friends who will see an older model."

"So, what's your advice? Wait until I've been here awhile or go for the Hollywood image of myself that I have in my heart?"

"Whatever you want. Every change can be made in a few seconds, and there's no limit on the number of changes."

"And people who knew us on Earth will continue to see us as we were back there? Does this image in their minds ever change?"

"Actually, it does. The final changes that you make (if you choose a final change) will be changed in their minds and hearts, too. Your final choice may take a couple centuries for you to decide. God encourages speeding up your decision if you hate your large nose or Dumbo ears that you have now. A person's Joy in Heaven is not lessened during the wait. The Joy just becomes more glorious when the change is complete."

"All I have to do is ask for a change? Can I experiment right now?"

"Sure. Go ahead."

"Then I wish that my waist would be the size that it was (32 inches) when I graduated from High School."

Then my pants fell down! Roger laughed so hard that the birds in a nearby elm stopped singing. Just uncontrollable laughter—finally he collapsed on the ground. Slightly upset, but still smiling (in Heaven, nobody gets too upset by humor or laughter, even at your expense), I reached down, pulled up my pants, and grudgingly said, "Pounds back on, please?" My fingers almost got caught as the fat flowed back into place. Roger caught his breath, hiccupped a few times, and stood up.

"Care to try that again or do you—?"

Roger was interrupted by a dazzling white light that appeared next to him. I could see that someone was inside the white light, only catching glimpses of a large figure in a snow-white gown, with a hawk embroidered on the front. The frightening person spoke in a deep bass voice.

"I don't know why hiccups attract me! Wherever I am, on Earth or in Heaven, I am drawn to the hiccup spot!"

Roger hiccupped, bowed slightly and whispered to me: "It's the Holy Spirit! Bow a bit!"

A chuckle rolled out from the misty figure, "Well, Roger, up to your old tricks, eh? Another Newcomer loses his pants."

Roger hiccupped.

"I wish that we hadn't suggested this as a way to brighten the days of our Heavenly Guides, but you know what a joker God the Father is."

Roger hiccupped.

"But no one's hurt, no hard feelings, and we've had a good laugh. I wish you'd ask God the Father about your hiccups, however, Roger."

And He was gone! Roger looked slightly embarrassed. He apologized to me.

"Sorry about that. Not the best way to meet the Holy Spirit. Normally, however, you'd be here a decade or two before you'd talk to one of the Big Three."

"I didn't. All I did was look foolish as I tried to hitch my pants back up and not faint! His voice is like comforting, rumbling thunder."

"Yeah. He's the sweetest one of the Holy Trio. More touchy-feely than the other two. I think He was a lot more careful about what He said than usual. You were so busy hauling up your pants that He didn't want to upset you any more. I'll try to be a little more cautious with my future hiccups. I had no idea that He was *drawn* to hiccups—just that He got them when He was upset."

"Back to business? I didn't know what we'd be learning once we got here. That's why I objected to playing the harp for all of Eternity. I could just hear it, over and over and over, forever and ever. It didn't occur to me that Brahms and Bach, Mozart and Handel would be writing new music after they got to Heaven. Or at least variations on what they'd written earlier. Is somebody in charge of the Heavenly harpists and choirs?"

"As a matter of fact, Mozart is a head choir conductor. He has other jobs, too. Rehearsing the Holy Harps, plus auditioning new members."

"Do you mean that some Newcomers are left out of the Holy Harps? What's Heavenly about that? Doesn't sound like the Joy of Heaven to me."

"Easy does it! If an applicant for the Holy Harps isn't good enough, that person can take additional lessons until he is good enough to be chosen."

"How long does that take? Don't some people get discouraged and just quit trying out?"

"Very few, actually. It's more a matter of wanting to be a harpist than inborn musical ability. Very often, the person who wants to be a harp player decides to go into a another area of performance, too. Wait until you hear some of the piano and violin soloists, plus singers. You think you heard some outstanding musicians on Earth? Wait until you hear the best that Heaven can offer. With everyone able to change from instrumental to vocal, music in Heaven brings Joy to all of us. Shakespeare's 'If music be the food of love, play on' has a larger, more emotional power in Heaven than on Earth. Just wait until you hear a favorite song or instrumental selection played in Heaven."

"It's already happening. When I first got to Heaven, I heard some faint sounds of harps. They sounded good."

"Any idea about why they sounded faint?"

"Because I didn't really think of Heavenly Harps as a treasure?"

"And because you hear more, the harps will become a more important part of your Heaven."

"I still don't want to be a harpist!"

"Not yet anyway. No rush. But maybe sometime in Future Eternity. Just wait until you hear the thousand-voiced Heavenly Choir. You're kind of a softie anyway, as music often brought tears to your eyes while you were on Earth. But you were so busy being a laid-back Lutheran that you're going to be frightened the first time the Tears of Joy flow down your face. You'll get used to it. We're very used to seeing men cry in Heaven. It's a good thing. Maybe that's one of the reasons that women adapt to Heaven more easily than men—women feel emotions sooner and stronger than men—they're used to crying. Unlike Earth, however, when the tears may have been from pain and suffering, now the tears are Tears of Joy."

"How often does the full Heavenly Choir perform? That must be a special occasion. What happens in Heaven that calls for such a celebration?"

"The most recent was the arrival of Mother Teresa. I was quite surprised at how well she reacted to Heaven. She wasn't bothered at all when the Big Three spoke to her. God the Father joked with her a little: 'We don't know quite how to welcome you. We've looked forward to your arrival for so long. Would you like an extra Guide or two?' She didn't miss a beat: 'Yes, I would. Make that six males, young and good-looking!' Everyone there roared with laughter, except God the Father. He just smiled broadly and nodded His head in reply. We're all encouraged to smile and laugh aloud in Heaven."

"This place is a lot more fun than I expected it to be!"

"God the Son took her hand and helped her into a carriage. She was still quite old and frail when she first got here. I don't know if she has changed her appearance since then. No member of the Holy Trinity makes a habit of touching any Newcomers in Heaven. Most of them would be so overcome, they'd just faint! Whenever any of the Big Three visits around in Heaven, each of them must cut back on the light and energy He produces."

"Did anything special happen later with Mother Teresa?"

"First, the Holy Spirit nodded to six of the handsomest Guides. We tend to move around in groups when not assigned to Newcomers. We're also integrated—half male and half female—although that isn't important in Heaven, rules being what they are. The chosen Guides were all tall, husky, handsome Hollywood types. We all smiled and shouted our approval as Mother Teresa's carriage drove off. The Holy Spirit floated along behind her carriage, obviously determined to make her feel at home. Mother Teresa now works with Newcomers who were starving and sickly on Earth, helping them to enjoy the First Fruits of Heaven, having enough to eat and being well. More about those unfortunate Newcomers later."

"And brevity still escapes us!"

"See, you're getting the hang of Heaven already—saying *us*, not only you."

"Things just seem to happen. Is that the way Heaven works?"

"Whatever God wants to happen makes Heaven work. No free will or anything to make it complicated. God has set up how things work in Heaven, and no human beings are strong enough to oppose God's will. That's how we got here in the first place—only by the Grace of God, not because of anything we believed or did."

"Amen, so be it! I'm beginning to accept the ways of Heaven, even though I don't always understand them."

"Good! Now back to what you can change about yourself in Heaven—plus *how* and *why*. You'll find that members of your family who are here will greet you warmly, hug you, and talk about old times. They do not cling to you, however. They are very busy with their own Heavenly work. Plus, they want to help you decide on what you want to do for Eternity."

"You mean that I won't be spending Eternity with my Earthly family and friends who are here in Heaven?"

"Probably not. One of the problems with our families on Earth was that they often became more important to us than God. Was that true in your life?"

"Yes, it was. But I felt that I was doing what God wanted me to do when I provided everything that I could for my wife and children."

"Did this lead you to putting your family first in using your Earthly time, talent, and money? Or did you put God and your neighbors first on Earth, before your family? Did you remember the commandment, 'You shall love the Lord your God with all your heart and your mind, and your neighbor as yourself'? Did you make the right decision—or was your decision a sin?"

"Yes, putting my family first was a sin. Although many people would argue that God gave us our families and expects us to take care of them. But I am forgiven, not because my intentions were good, but entirely by the Grace of God."

"Both of us now see the sin in in putting our families first?"

"Yes, and I'm sorry. May God forgive me."

"He already has."

There was a short pause while I gave myself time to accept an idea that my brain (logic) accepted but that my heart (feelings) still struggled with. Finally, I said, "On a lighter note: what about some changes in my physical appearance?"

"I suggest that you wait until we talk more, until you look around more in Heaven. Make an immediate change of your clothes for the simple robe that most of the Newcomers in Heaven wear. It's comfortable, won't fall down the way your pants did, and will make you easy to identify as a Newcomer when you meet new folks in Heaven."

"How easier? Is the robe magic?"

"Not magic at all! We don't approve of magic stuff here in Heaven. Your robe will be a fashionable light green in color. The light green tells persons who meet you that you're a Newcomer to Heaven and will need simple stuff explained to you because you haven't been here long."

"Will I be wearing this green thing for quite a while?"

"Easy, easy! The green robe will look better than you think. Let's do it." Roger pointed to my body. "New robe to wear, let it be there! Well, how do you like it?"

"Really nice! Comfortable, an attractive color, lightweight. But won't this light color show dirt and food stains?"

"You forget that this is Heaven—no dirt or sweat—and wrinkle-free. Food stains won't be a problem for you. Are you hungry?"

"No, I'm not. But I've only been in Heaven for a few hours, I think. My watch has stopped."

"As well it might. Earth time is gone: welcome to happy Eternity! You won't need to eat. You arrived here with a full belly and more than a little excess body fat. For those who arrived here starved, undernourished, weak from lack of food, Heaven has plenty of food. God has even set up a special program for these victims of constant hunger on Earth. They receive all they can eat of the foods they ate on Earth for as long as they feel hunger. Most of them no longer feel hunger after a few weeks although a few skinny individuals will continue eating, never overeating, for nearly a year. Satisfied by what they have eaten, these Newcomers develop new interests in Heaven and no longer desire food."

"So what happens to the food program? And who is responsible for raising, processing, and preparing the food?"

"No need to worry about hungry people—we receive thousands of them every day. With the world's population explosion, the number of starving people has continued to increase. You saw regularly on TV about the starving people in Sudan, Ethiopia, and other places on Earth. Here in Heaven, volunteers provide the necessary work force. The planters, harvesters, preparers, servers, and clean-up crews are usually city men and women who never needed to work outdoors on Earth. Why? Perhaps because no one is telling them to do these chores. It is one way of loving your neighbors in Heaven. And working outdoors they enjoy perfect weather. (It's always Heavenly here.) "

"And, because it's Heaven, no cold water, snakes, and bugs in the rice paddies? I imagine bumper crops are always the rule?"

"Of course! God doesn't miss an opportunity to multiply his Earthly blessings when they are transferred to Heaven."

"A final question on eating. I'm a little embarrassed to ask. What about digestion, going to the bathroom, and all the plumbing connected with eating?"

"You've done it again! Give God a little credit. Through a special process, at first, food will fill out the bodies of the hungry people, with any leftover energy being released into the air to be used by the trees, grass, and flowers which you see here in Heaven. I don't know exactly how it works, but you can see the results around you."

"Some of the trees are gigantic! They make Earth's Giant Sequoias look like saplings."

"Of course. This is Heaven. Bigger and better than Texas."

"Are these trees ever cut down to make lumber?"

"No. God has other short-cut methods to provide any building materials needed."

"A final question: what about the young people, even infants, who die before they experience childhood, do they have a chance to become a grown-up?"

"God has thought of that, too. If the child dies and the mother is still alive on Earth, God provides someone who looks and even smells like the child's mother to take care of the young person until the child matures (to about 18 years of age). If the Earth mother dies before the child matures, she steps into the place of her substitute. Neither the mother nor the child is aware of the substitution. This gives each child a chance to grow up being loved by its mother (or substitute) and playing with other children, learning to share both toys and favorite blankets. Each child learns 'It is better to give than to receive' and other useful ideas about life which will make them healthy, happy adults. The Trinity spent a lot of time in setting up a program that turns children into adults who can make Heaven even better than it is now."

"Should you tell me more about what my body will look like in Heaven?"

"I could—and I probably will tell you later, particularly about how your brain will also be improved. Incidentally, how's your waistline doing?"

"Wow! I'm not the 32" that I was when I graduated from High School, but I'm getting there. I'm improving! Look out, Heaven—here I come!"

"Easy does it. Take your time. You'll be able to make any further changes in your body at any time. Ready for the next Amendment?"

Chapter 5

The New Dimension
(OR "Now You See It—Now It's Changed!")

"The Third Amendment: 'At first, what you see and hear in Heaven will be what you expected Heaven to be. This Heaven will change.' What's the big deal about that? On Earth, one of first things that we learn is 'Things change!' We're used to change. A new house. A new car. A new job. A new friend. A new Special Other. Your first girlfriend preferred the high school football star. You earned a full college scholarship. Your parents divorced. Your favorite grandmother died suddenly. How did you react to these changes?"

"Some changes made me very happy; others made me sad. Some changes took years to accept; others were never forgiven or forgotten. I shed tears of joy—and tears of anger and sadness. That was part of living on Earth. I managed to deal with all those changes, although not always well."

"That's where Heaven is better than Earth. You learn to accept the changes you need to make to live in Heaven. But there are no tears, only joy! You've heard of a win-win situation? Well, Heaven is it!"

"As I remember, when I first came to Heaven, everything was unclear, kind of blurry. The monogram P on St. Peter's robe helped me identify him. I remember the tent, then the two other people in the tent, and finally, a grassy area outside the tent, ringed by trees, mostly oaks and elms."

"The reason that you saw Heaven more clearly after a while here was that you didn't have a very definite idea of what Heaven would be like while on Earth."

"Yes, and the always-present light of Heaven, soothing and not too bright, made me relax, with a feeling of peace and joy in my heart—this was Heaven! Living here kept getting better and better. The ideas that you shared changed me, with no hint of criticism. Your concern was simply to help me."

"Are you ready for more?"

"Sure! I already know that I'll visit Hell but won't want to stay there. That I will see my family members who got to Heaven before I did, although probably briefly and only temporarily. What other choices do I have?"

"Your choices in Heaven will continue to multiply from now on into Eternity. Plus, you can always go back and choose an earlier alternative to the one you just made. Every choice will make you more secure, happier. You will make no bad choices, only better choices—for all Eternity! Are you ready?"

"No more physical changes in me for right now. Somehow, my waist has shrunk back to the 32 inches which I last owned in high school! How did that happen? Did you cheat and give me an unexpected gift in Heaven? Were you the one who surprised me with a physical change in Heaven? Is that allowed?"

"Yes, I did ask for a smaller waist for you. We are not encouraged to make this kind of change, but if it helps to cheer up Newcomers, make them happier, more able to make the needed changes in Heaven, the Guide's request is allowed. If not, only the Guide and God know. And God is pretty liberal with such gifts. By the way, 'liberal' is still a good word in Heaven if not always a positive word on Earth. Yes, God is liberal with His Grace--and we need every bit of it that we can get! Maybe God the Father planned for you to be embarrassed when your pants fell down."

"I hadn't thought of that. Does God the Father have a sense of humor about stuff like that?"

"He likes broad humor. But always with mild consequences. Not like on Earth. Moving on: what kind of work would you like to try out before you decide on your Heavenly work choice?"

"I'm not sure. Do you go with me while I look around and begin to make some decisions?"

"Absolutely. I won't leave you until we both agree that it's the thing to do."

"Should I try to understand Heaven better by visiting people in Heaven who are different in color or religion? Is that the right road?"

"It's not the only road. I think you're ready for a short cut, although time isn't a big issue in Eternity. But the sooner you know more, choose more, change more, the sooner you will receive your full reward of peace and joy in Heaven. You could listen to God's options for your work in Eternity right now."

"Do you think that I'm ready?"

"In choosing your work for Eternity the three areas of interest are physical labor, computer jobs, and education/fine arts (including language study and literature). One of our continuing jobs in Heaven is to provide food to the Newcomers who are hungry, even starving to death while on Earth. When they come to Heaven, we give them what they were familiar with on Earth—basic foods such as rice, wheat, potatoes, plus vegetables, fruits, and other side dishes. The time it takes for Newcomers to give up eating in Heaven varies a great deal. Surprisingly, a majority of these hungry Newcomers stop eating after a week or two of having enough food. Some take months, even years to wean themselves off the eating habit. On the other hand, some individuals simply grasp more quickly than others that the time of food shortage is over, no longer important. Much depends on how long these people were short of food."

"But why the continued need to feed hungry people?"

"With the increasing population on Earth, the number of hungry Newcomers is increasing day by day. As you know, 50% of the people on Earth go to sleep hungry every night."

"But God could help these hungry Newcomers to forget their Earthly hunger in some way, couldn't He?"

"Of course. But not only does this temporary food plan finally give some of Earth's people a chance to fill their stomachs, but it gives some indoor job holders a chance to work outside. The secretaries, teachers, and computer operators have a different type of work, being outdoors. They are reminded of the continued need for equal distribution of food on Earth. They've done sitting work. Now they prefer to do physical labor in Heaven. Besides, in Heaven, physical work doesn't even make you sweat! It's more like fun, not sweat and tears as work is on Earth."

"So that's how hungry Newcomers adjust to Heaven?"

"The individual's idea of Heaven changes, too. Each Newcomer learns that a better Heaven will result from each person's 'work,' an activity which brings more joy because each person does God's work, right in His house."

"Will the work be something we like to do?"

"Absolutely! In every case. Chances are that the work will not be what you did on Earth, although it might be related."

"How do we learn new skills, new ways of life in Heaven?"

"Aha! The professor in you comes out again. Yes, there are classes in which you learn new skills hands-on instead of from lectures. And, yes, God could have made this learning an instant change, automatic. But He knew from His experiences with the people from Earth that they are happiest when they are doing something, not just listening to someone telling them how to do it. Newcomers are happier and learn faster when they practice the skill they're learning—even if it has to be repeated over and over. However, this being Heaven, learning comes easily, so most people learn very well in their first attempt. Occasionally, the process is repeated a second time, but seldom beyond that."

"Who chooses to do what? Is there any pattern?"

"The pattern seems to be that the work will be very different from what the person did on Earth. For instance, Albert Einstein has become a gardener as his life work in Heaven. Even as a child, he loved flowers, but now he enjoys a physically active, outdoor type of work, developing new varieties of roses, gladiolas, daisies, and other flowers. The sizes, colors, and fragrances of the flowers are, well, Heavenly. If you liked flowers on Earth, you'll love them in Heaven."

"Can you give me a sample of what Heavenly flowers look like?"

"Certainly! Just a moment."

Roger turned away from me, blocking my view of some bushes I hadn't noticed a moment ago. He stooped, plucked some flowers, still keeping them out of my sight, then, grinning, he turned to me. In his right hand were three roses—larger, more beautiful, and even from several feet away, more fragrant than any rose I'd ever seen or smelled on Earth. One was red, shading to a deeper scarlet at the center of the fringed petals, occasionally showing light streaks of a brilliant pink at the outer edges. The yellow was pure in color, but with splashes of gold that only a sunset could suggest. The yellow petals were huge, like a gentle sparkling waterfall. The white rose was so perfect that I felt that I was looking into the love of God Himself. Still, I glimpsed bits of color, reminding me of the rainbow, even the entire universe. I sank to my knees in the grass, then held out my right hand hesitantly. Roger crossed over to me, handing the roses to me, one by one. I looked at Roger's gentle smile as tears streamed down my cheeks. I arranged the three roses in my left hand, then grasped them in both hands and held them to my chest.

"You'll notice—no thorns."

"Did these roses come from Einstein's bushes?"

"Yes, but they grow in God's garden."

I nodded my understanding, stood up, and offered the roses back to Roger. I couldn't hold them any longer. They were too powerful for me to keep in my hands. Roger looked down a path to his right. Three nearly-teenage children chased one another along the path, playing tag. When they came up to us, they stopped and bowed to each of us. Roger offered each of them a single rose. They looked at their roses, held them out for the others to see and smell. Then each spoke softly and lovingly to the flowers they held. Again, they bowed to us and ran, overjoyed with their new-found treasures, down the path to our left. I had regained some of my calm, so I cleared my throat, and smiled at Roger, blowing my nose before I spoke.

"Please, if you're going to show me any other wonderful things in Heaven, at least give me a hint first. I may be able to control myself better."

"No, the joys of Heaven will overwhelm you, regardless of what I might do. And it's good for you to cry as you're a typical stiff-necked Lutheran. In Heaven, we encourage you to cry. After all, in Heaven you will have only tears of joy. However, next time I'll try to warn you."

"Einstein must be so proud of his roses. They bring joy to anyone who sees and smells them."

"Einstein has many other flowers, too. God encourages Einstein to experiment in producing new varieties of bigger and better flowers. In fact, God had to suggest to Einstein that too big could be a problem. Other people had to help Einstein tie up his blooms and support the huge flowers with special nets and holders. When what one person does in Heaven makes work for others up here, God usually calls a halt to bigger and better, and not just in growing flowers. People in Heaven often work together, but what they work on is of major interest to all of them."

We stood quietly for a moment while I caught my emotional breath. With an embarrassed clearing of my throat, I asked Roger another question.

"You told me earlier that Einstein played poker fairly often with Stalin, Hitler, and Freud. So people in Heaven don't work all the time?"

"No, they don't. God thinks that work, with equal time for Recreation, is a good plan for the citizens of Heaven. On Earth, we worked eight hours a day, five days a week in the developed countries. That leaves most evenings and weekends, plus national holidays and vacations, for fun, Recreation, what we like to do because it gives us pleasure—and, in a number of cases, physical exercise. Citizens of Heaven choose the type of work they want to do, but also their Recreation."

One Man's Heaven

"Do a majority of Newcomers choose a type of work that seldom changes? Is this what pleases God the most?"

"God doesn't care. As long as the individual is happy in the work being done, God is pleased. Only about 10% of the Newcomers stay in their original jobs. Usually people who had a strong work ethic on Earth feel uncomfortable changing jobs when they first get here. Often these people who have trouble making changes are Germans and Scandinavians, especially if they're Lutheran. The amusing result for these folks is that after they see that Heaven is all about change, they loosen up and go wild, making up to a dozen different job changes in a year. After that, they're like the majority of the Newcomers, who change jobs every year or two, right on into Eternity."

"Is there any individual who set a record by staying in his first job for a long time?"

"Yes, there is. A rather sad case, actually. God fretted about this man for nearly ten years because he stayed in the same job. God assigned two Guides to this man, allowing them to bring in other experts to help, too. It was the closest God ever came to breaking His own Rules about changes. God won't just step in and make the person change. God has infinite patience, but even He learned other ways to get a stubborn Newcomer to accept the freedom and joy of making changes. God learned that the slow changer did better, became faster in accepting the changes of Heaven, if that person was included in a mixed group of at least six people—three easy changers and three slow changers, including the problem Newcomer. Two Guides would still be used at the same time with the Group Change Project, but Guides were free to ask for replacements at any time."

"How did that all work out?"

"Pretty well. Crazy Adam was an unusual case, a hard case. He held out against change for almost ten years. He was a Medieval monk who stood on one leg for over 20 years in an isolated mountain range in what is now Iran. How he got started, how he managed to survive the heat and cold, the hunger, no one knew. He stood on a cliff which could be seen by the camel caravans as they came by on a trail only a hundred yards from where Adam stood above them. Everyone stopped, gave Adam food and water and talked to him. Yes, he had to get down on both legs occasionally—to answer calls of nature, pick up food stored nearby, grab an extra robe in cold weather, and so on. But, basically, he stood on one leg (switching from right to left as necessary) for almost 20 years. He did not wash himself or his clothes. To say he was caked with dirt was an understatement. But he remained cheerful, talked to any visitors who climbed up to him with food and water. But, most importantly to him, he stood on either one leg or the other. He could close off his consciousness to the cold or heat, rain or hail, baking sun or freezing darkness. He forgot why he started the standing on one leg business. He made the vow when his younger brother, only eight, looked as if he was dying of a raging fever. Crazy Adam promised God that if his brother lived, Adam would stand on one leg in an isolated place on a distant mountain for the rest of his life."

"What did God think of this standing on one leg business? Did He feel that this strange position was a good way for Adam to worship Him?"

"No, God did not approve, but he had a rule that didn't allow Him to interfere with a person's choice on Earth. Man would learn to accept the results of his actions on Earth. Only in Heaven would every person be rewarded with the joys of Heaven, being with God."

"Whatever happened to Adam? Obviously, his brother lived, as Adam fulfilled his vow."

"Yes, Adam's young brother, John, recovered and became a leader in his tribe. Everyone in the village and in the surrounding area knew Adam's story. Despite the distance away from Adam's home, over 100 miles of dangerous mountain paths and trails, someone brought food and water to Adam every week."

"For nearly 20 years. Amazing! Both how Adam stood on one leg and that his friends and family took food and water to him for all those years."

"Yes, God approved of that. Maybe the long-range care of Adam reminded the givers of God's law that you give to those in need."

"Whatever happened to Adam? How did he die?"

"As the years went on, Adam became weaker and weaker. One night, during a wild windstorm, Adam could no longer hold onto his leaning post, which helped him to stand on one leg. The wind pushed him until, still fighting the wind, still erect, he fell off his cliff to the rocks below. His family, particularly his brother, John, was worried about him, got there about noon and found him dead below the cliff. They buried him near his 'leaning post,' feeling that Adam would want to be buried near his strange home. God agreed and decided to give crazy Adam special care as soon as he got to Heaven."

"And how did that finally turn out?"

"Adam has great powers of concentration, is very intelligent, and likes people. When Adam accepted the idea of change, he outdid himself. One of Adam's Guides played various board games with him—chess, checkers, Scrabble, Monopoly. Adam was so quick in learning to play each game and in winning every time that soon no one would play games with him. At this point, God Himself stepped in. He suggested that Adam's Heavenly work should be teaching others in Heaven how to play board games and how to be a winner. This worked really well–now there are hundreds of thousands of people in Heaven who have learned to play board games as a part of their Recreation. Adam still enjoys teaching, but God has to lean on a couple of Angels to get them to play chess with Adam. The Angels are really smart and, sometimes they almost beat Adam. God refuses to play."

"After hearing the Adam story, I feel there may be hope for me."

"Oh, you're no great problem. How do you feel about making changes, especially in Heaven? I think I know what you'll say."

"I'm all for changes, especially when there's no penalty for making mistakes or a limit to the number of changes I can make. Heaven is a lot better than I expected. Even—"

"Let's not get back to the Angels and harps again, O.K.? I believe you're even changing on that subject."

"I am. I hear more and more harp music, the longer I'm here. And it sounds louder, clearer, and more pleasing the longer I listen. This is part of my seeing and hearing Heaven as it is, rather than what I vaguely expected, isn't it? God is giving me time to adjust to Heaven gradually."

"Yep, but not only you. God gives all the Newcomers time to adjust to Heaven as it really is, not just as you imagined. As I mentioned, Einstein took less than a week with his Personal Guide before he accepted the main ideas of Heaven and knew how he would need to change his mind and actions to be entirely at home in Heaven."

"And I'm no Einstein, right? Don't even answer that. Back to our earlier discussion on Newcomers choosing Heavenly work and Heavenly play, changing whenever they want to. Is someone keeping a record of all these changes? Sounds like a mess to me."

"Oh, somebody's in charge of recording all the changes, all right. In the Old Days, each person of the Trinity took turns in supervising the recording of work/play/vacation times for each Newcomer in Heaven. Sort of a Good Book of Heavenly Activities, rather than the Book of bad deeds on Earth that we're all familiar with. Fortunately, that's an Earthly myth that all persons can forget when they die. The original Book never existed—it was only one of man's feeble attempts to understand God and Heaven."

"Both God and Heaven are more forgiving, kinder, and more loving than Newcomers have ever been able to imagine, right?"

"Hang onto that! Back to keeping Heavenly records. By adapting modern computers for Heavenly use, a trained group of Angels split up the responsibility for Newcomer traffic from different geographical areas, which is almost completely automatic in adding each person as he dies and comes to Heaven, then noting work/play/vacation times and changes in each program."

"Geographical areas? Are there directions in Heaven? Are continents handled separately?"

"Continents, no; directions, yes. Just north, south, east, and west. Only the East is split up into two regions. With both China and India in that area, a majority of Newcomers arrive from that direction; twice as many computers are used in this region as in all the other regions put together."

"Sounds complicated."

"God has made it so simple that you and I could be of help if we were needed."

"Speak for yourself, Roger! I could barely get into and out of e-mail on our computer on Earth."

"In Heaven all things are possible, even making you computer literate."

"I hope we don't have to test your belief in my ability to change my mind about computers."

"Actually, the 100 Angels trained in this special computer work are split into two groups. Each 50 Angels is on for a week, then off for a week, for an entire year. God trained the first group of 100 Angels himself—the only One with enough knowledge about the program to set it up on computers rather than the loose-leaf notebooks they'd been using. What a mess! It took only two weeks, however, to convert to computer use and to switch the previous notebook material to the computer files. God had some secret way of doing this, which really speeded up the transfer. However, God never told anyone, other than the other Two of the Big Three how He did it. Probably too difficult for us to understand anyway. Where were we? Oh, yes! The Asians in Heaven are now in the majority, have been for many years."

"Does God divide Earth's Newcomers by color and religion when they get to Heaven?"

"Only at first. Then as Newcomers get used to Heaven, they begin to mix with those who are different from themselves in color, religion or whatever. Within an Earth year or two, everybody's pretty well mixed together."

"I expected Heaven to be like Earth in how we worship God—lots of prayers, singing, praising God, and asking Him for forgiveness. That doesn't seem to be what God has in mind, in Heaven, from what I've seen and heard so far."

"No, but Luther had it pretty close to right when he said that all our work (and play) can serve as worship to God and our fellow man, if the things we do are positive and joyful."

"Wish I'd gotten that message sooner--when I was still on Earth. No, thinking about that comment again, I (like all my neighbors, all my brothers and sisters) was too self-centered to be anything other than a hopeful sinner. And the hopeful note was a good idea."

"So Heaven hasn't turned out to be the way you expected the Kingdom of God to be?"

"I thought that Heaven would be spent doing the things that I liked to do on Earth. Maybe golfing, fishing, card-playing (from solitaire to bridge)."

"God tried that idea some thousands of years ago with Cave People. But those folks just wanted to go on picking wild berries and harvesting wild rice, storing it up for later use. To most of us, harvesting berries and rice were too much like work on Earth, although their fishing struck a happy chord with us. However, after being in Heaven for a century or two, the Cave People wanted to do something more to help them enjoy the true Joy of Heaven. So God obliged with His work/fun/vacation plan, which, with minor improvements, is still in effect today. God does good work."

"The whole idea of Heaven seems to be working. I've never seen so many smiling faces. So, for them, Heaven is as good as they'd hoped it would be. For me, it's even better. Of course, being Lutheran, I guess that I wasn't very hopeful or imaginative."

"For most of us, Heaven is better than we had hoped it would be. More joy, more forgiveness, more love. We're all different, but we're all in this together. God has made Heaven a rich, unexpected reward. Now we do our part to help Him make Heaven even better!"

"So where are we in my orientation?"

"We just finished with the Third Amendment. It reminds you that what we see and hear in Heaven will be pretty much what we expected—at first. Then you were reminded that you would need to make changes in your beliefs and attitudes in order to find the full Joy of Heaven."

"But the changes are so logical and well thought-out that they were easily accepted. No problems so far."

"That's because God is so good at His job, making Heaven more wonderful than we had hoped for or expected."

"Right! So on we go to Amendment Four!"

Chapter 6

Do You Choose Heaven, Earth, Or Hell?
(OR "Is There Really a Choice?")

"Amendment Four: 'Not long after you get to Heaven, you will choose whether you wish to remain in Heaven, return to Earth, or go to Hell. You may visit Hell at any time, returning to Heaven whenever you want. Few people remain in Hell very long.' "

"Why would anyone want to visit Hell anyway?"

"Curiosity. Or you might want to see if the bully who kicked your butt across Main Street almost every morning on your way to First Grade is there."

"He waited for me at the only school crossing on the fairly busy Main Street in Sauk Centre. I don't know why Brownie picked on me (skinny, small?). He waited behind me until the crossing guard stopped the traffic, then he kicked my butt three or four times as I hurried across the street. It didn't hurt much, but it was embarrassing. Luckily for me, Brownie, who was only a grade or two ahead of me, but bigger and definitely meaner, missed a lot of school. I hated going to school. I blushed easily in those days—I'm sure that I lit up like a ripe tomato all the way across the street. No one ever tried to help me or even yell at him. And I was too scared to say anything to my teacher. Where was God when I needed Him?"

"He was there. Watching and hoping that you'd protest, strike out at Brownie—do something. Maybe this helped you in some way to solve similar problems when you grew up. What finally happened with Brownie?"

"Before the year ended, he and his family moved to California. Years later I heard that Brownie, then a teenager, had died in a motorcycle accident. I knew that God wouldn't approve of my response to Brownie's death: I was glad that he got his. He deserved it."

"God smiled a bit at your reaction, forgave you at once, but ruined your possibility of seeing Brownie in Hell. Actually, he just stayed here in Heaven without even visiting the Lower Depths."

"How do you know all this?"

"When a Newcomer begins to tell his Guide a story about his life on Earth, the Guide presses a New Info button. The machine checks the details and accuracy of the story, reporting the results to the Guide. It's a remarkable computer program that God worked out about 50 years ago. Now the computer Angels put the information about each person's life on Earth into the computer system. Your story was relatively accurate."

"But God let Brownie into Heaven without any fuss?"

"Yes, He did. Brownie's life on Earth had been difficult. Brownie had nine brothers and sisters, so his parents, both working more than one job to provide food, clothing, and housing for their children, did not have time to pay attention to Brownie, one of their oldest children. On his own, Brownie got in with the wrong friends, into trouble with the police, and died while being chased after a store holdup."

"Did I do something wrong? Should I have encouraged him to kick me harder, more often?"

"No, of course not. Brownie was only directing his anger at the world by kicking you. It's the old Kick the Cat idea, very popular on Earth. You were just the convenient target. Do you forgive Brownie now?"

"I forgave him years ago. But it took a while. I was in Senior High already. The hate for Brownie that I had to carry around was just too big a load with the additional baggage I was carrying by then. I guess I was probably a sophomore when I forgave Brownie."

"The anger was gone. You felt better, right?"

"Right. Moving on?"

"Most people don't even think of leaving Heaven once they get here. Many of them are quite surprised they made it. Heaven pleases them so much they don't want to press their luck. A majority of them, even if they have heard of The Grace of God, couldn't really accept it or even understand it. Most of them had been taught you get what you deserve, what you must pay for. And they didn't want that, thank you very much! Hell would be the logical destination if they didn't have God's Grace. But they had the key to Heaven. After a sincere "Thank You, God!" each Newcomer began to work his way through the 10 Amendments, ready to help God make Heaven even better."

"A majority of Newcomers see God's goal that quickly and easily?"

"Yes—remember who set all this up. God knows what He's doing. But we win the prize. Regardless of their Earthly belief in a particular God, once Newcomers get to Heaven, all differences are erased. Whether the One God of Jews and Moslems, the more debatable Trinity-Yet-One God of Christians, the many gods of the Egyptians, Greeks, Romans, Hindus, Buddhists and other religions, or the God-in-Nature (Earth, wind, animals, etc.) of native tribes through all the Earth. And each society sets up its own non-religious gods."

"You mean like our American worship of the family? Or just money? The things that money can buy—an expensive home, a fancy car, a good school for our kids? We don't put God first in our lives. Maybe second or even third? Or we simply believe in ourselves to the point that we give ourselves all the credit for our successes? We become our own God? Materialism and secularism, leaving God out and putting things or ourselves first—this becomes our religious belief. So when we get here, Heaven is a shock for us. But God gives us as long as we need to get from confused Newcomers to Heavenly old timers?"

"Who's the Guide here anyway? Or did you always want to be a pastor, a minister?"

"Nope, I never did. It's too hard to sell something that can't be seen or touched. And I've always been too busy judging, telling my neighbors why they're wrong, to be of much help to them, even in a sermon on a Sunday."

"One of the troubles with somebody who's made it—a career or a family or a nest egg or all of these things—is that they feel that if they can do it, so can others. Pull themselves up by their own bootstraps, get off welfare, live in a decent part of town. Too often, we forget the advantages that we've had—family help for a college education, some breaks in our careers or marriage or family-raising. How often did we come close to making the wrong decision, doing the wrong thing? Or having good health, which you were smart enough or lucky enough to keep by proper eating and exercise. How come you did the right thing? No crippling disease or car accident? Maybe Somebody Else gave you a helping hand, but you didn't see it. God does help us—and we, in turn, need to help one another."

"You don't have to preach to me. I agree. But many among us do not even believe in Heaven. I die, I'm buried, I push up daisies."

"When we find ourselves in Heaven, we need to have a quick look at Hell first. Just to see what the other choice is. Hell can be pretty attractive to us at first—Dante got it wrong. But when we visit Hell we feel no joy, no love, no presence of God in our lives. So we take the quick route back to Heaven! We don't just run, we fly! We accept the 10 Amendments at once and become permanent residents of Heaven for Eternity."

"What is there in Hell that would tempt a Newcomer to stay there, even for a while?

"Do you want to go down there and see for yourself?"

"Would you go with me?"

"If you want me to, I can. But you are allowed to go alone—you'd be perfectly safe. God and His Angels are still watching over you—even in Hell."

"I'd like you to go along with me, Roger. I'm still a little scared, even of Heaven. It's almost too much for me, especially being a Lutheran. But the Joy of Heaven is growing in me just by being here."

"Don't worry about being a little scared of being in Heaven—that's not unusual. Yes, I'll go to Hell with you. It's a quick trip there and back. Or we can stay awhile. O.K.?"

"Yup. I'm still not as brave as I'd like to be, but my knees have stopped shaking. Can we take a slow route?"

We went down through fleecy sweet-smelling clouds that evaporated as we came to them. In Heaven, earlier, I caught a whiff of home-baked bread, followed by the sweet aroma of blooming roses, later a hint of my wife's Chanel #5 (used only sparingly or on special occasions). Roger smiled knowingly at me. "God is helping you to put Heaven farther from your mind." It was getting warmer around us; the light was brighter, causing me to squint. Then we were out of the clouds, drifting slowly to something that looked like Earth. But the trees weren't green at all—instead they were red, yellow, blue, even purple! Quite unattractive, even gaudy. The undersides of all the leaves were silver or gold, tinkling in the slight breeze. I didn't notice the buildings until we were nearly on the ground: copper, bronze, platinum and other metallic colors criss-crossed and zig-zagged up, down, over, and around the high rises ahead of us.

"Roger, where are the burning pits, the chin-high water, the screams of pain and suffering?"

Roger answered dryly, "Where they've always been, in the minds of imaginative poets like Dante, in his *Inferno*. What may have begun with fear in his soul went on to become the wonderful word pictures of what Hell might may be like. The words inspired the famous drawings and paintings of later times (particularly of the Medieval period). The real trouble with Hell is that it doesn't get any better, as Heaven already has for you. Instead, Hell will only look cheaper, less appealing, the longer you look at it."

"Or we make our own Hell-on-Earth, which often begins as the heavy ball that we carry around in the pits of our stomachs because of some angry or mean or cruel act that we have done or just thought. But oh, the time and the energy we waste punishing ourselves and others. We're so busy building walls and fences that we don't have enough time to appreciate the joys of Earth!"

Roger just smiled. "But now you can see the Hell of Eternal Punishment as just a place to visit. Not that everyone who visits Hell finds it too bad—there's good food, good golf, even good sex—for a while. Then the visitors see Hell for what it is. A temporary place of good things—but those good things are not enough. Heaven is your Eternal Home. But we're here. Should we give Hell a whirl?"

"Sure. I hope to see something new."

What struck me about Hell were the three types of people here. The largest number of looked like us—dressed in the different colored robes of Heaven. We were just spectators. The air in Hell had many different scents and smells, varying from my Mother's bread baking to the cold, clear air of a Minnesota winter night, changing so rapidly that I felt slightly dizzy. The Devil was trying hard to make me and the other Newcomers think about good things on Earth, promising them to us in Hell. Anything to try to make us forget Heaven. But his tricks didn't work—the Joy of Heaven was firmly in all our hearts and minds.

Sounds from Earth also played in our ears. Each of us heard favorite music from classical, popular, country-western, or some other type of orchestral or vocal composition from our past on Earth. Even Roger sang aloud some moving parts of a rather jazzed-up version of the hymn, *On Our Way Rejoicing*. In my own ear, I heard a familiar sonata of J. S. Bach, played joyously and full-volume on a huge organ by (Could it be? It was!) E. Power Biggs in Salt Lake City's Mormon Temple. Later, Roger told me that it was not unusual for visitors to join in their favorite fun in Hell, taking part in all the temptations that Hell offered. And the Devil knew each individual's weak spot—sex, gambling, drinking, gossiping (whatever turned them on while they were on Earth). However, even being caught up in the nets of vice in Hell, the desire to stay weakened in a day or two, a week, or occasionally as long as a year. They all returned to the joy of Heaven, being with God.

One Man's Heaven

I asked Roger later about the sins the Newcomers had committed while in Hell—did God punish them? Roger just smiled, saying, "Trust in the infinite Grace of God. The Devil is crafty but never as wise or forgiving as God."

Roger reminded me, that, as with Heaven, each Newcomer has a different idea of what Hell would be like. And God let us begin with what we believed and then find out something new about Hell. For many Newcomers, their first scenes of Hell included naked people twisted in pain and screaming in agony as tongues of flame licked at their bodies. Others saw people frozen, half in ice, half out, crying loudly because of their punishment. So this second group showed how people were punished in Hell.

However, not everyone expected Dante's Hell. Some, especially the more modern Newcomers, saw tanned, athletic men and women with trim bodies in tight swimwear that left little to the imagination as they dived, sipped cool drinks, and looked like romantic movie stars. Faces and bodies were reminders of Marilyn Monroe and Clark Gable. Their tans glistened in the sun as they swam in the pools or relaxed in their beach wear. These pretty faces and bodies drew sighs and low whistles from some of us Newcomers. The Devil was on the job, providing magical costumes and subtracting pounds from our overweight bodies. But this change did not work well. The Newcomers who joined the third kind of people in Hell, the Residents, looked more life-like than the pretty people in bathing suits. We all noticed that the Devil's people moved and talked more like robots or machines than human beings.

I asked Roger, "Is the Devil running out of regular citizens in Hell?"

"Yes, he is. The number of permanent residents dropped 7.5% from just a year ago. The decrease has been steady for over two centuries now. In fact, the Devil has so few permanent residents that he must use robots to fill in the showplaces. When the Newcomers get close to the robots, the machine-like quality in their movements and speech clearly prove that they are only machines."

"So what's the long-term result? Is the Devil going out of business?"

"Possibly. Only God knows."

"What would the Devil do then?"

"I don't know. There's been some talk about the Devil returning to Heaven to be with God again."

"Boy, that would that be a switch. How would our Earth people react?"

"Probably slowly. Earthlings would almost certainly continue to believe in the old Devil and Hell. Changes in beliefs, even good changes, go very slowly on Earth. God understands this and makes allowances for Earthlings' trouble with changing, especially ideas. Fewer and fewer people are even visiting Hell nowadays. Only about 1% of the Newcomers even bother to see what Hell is like. Plus fewer and fewer Newcomers choose to stay in Hell even briefly because they felt the need to be punished before they could return to Heaven."

"Does God agree with them? Are they punished?"

"Only by themselves. God's Grace has already forgiven them for their sins. Now, they're the only ones who feel that they must be punished."

"How long do most of them stay? Is there a record for time spent in Hell? Is the average more or less than earlier in history?"

"The average time spent in Hell (not counting the majority of the Newcomers, who visit and then leave the same day) is now about 7.5 days, down from an average of nearly three weeks during the 1800s."

"What's the reason for the change?"

"We Guides in Heaven think that we've learned to explain God's Forgiveness and Grace better than the Guides did centuries ago. The Holy Trinity also developed better communication methods. We Guides have regular retraining sessions as new ideas about learning have been developed."

"Does any idea or technique of learning seem more successful lately?"

"Yes, and it was a surprise to most of us Guides. The problem is the interpretation of Free Will and Salvation for quite a few of our Newcomers to Heaven. They were upset when they found Universal Salvation among the required 10 Amendments, which are necessary to be accepted as a permanent resident in Heaven. If everyone is saved from Hell, where's the Free Will? If God knew ahead of time that all people would make it to Heaven, why did we bother to go to church or temple regularly, to tithe to the church on Earth, and to help all of those in need. Free Will, to accept or reject God's offer of Salvation, did not seem to exist any more."

"Did you have an answer for these Free Will Newcomers?"

"Sort of. First, we learned to reply quietly and sympathetically that we understood why they were upset. But our answer was that God's Will is more powerful than Man's Free Will. So if God wants all persons to be saved—and He does—we must accept that God's Will is more powerful than our Free Will. The Grace of God erases all of man's sins. As a result, all mankind goes to an Eternity of Heaven. God asks us to remind all the Newcomers that if they want to go to Hell, they may do so. But God encourages the Newcomers to rejoin Him in Heaven at any time. No questions asked. Too many of us recall how our parents told us that in life you get what you deserve. Most of us, knowing our own faults and sins, said to ourselves, I hope not! And God says, 'Your hope has been answered. Welcome to Eternal Life in Heaven.'"

"God has even given us the option of Hell to sort out our ideas before accepting Universal Salvation. Thanks be to God!"

"Amen! Amen! Amen!"

"Is there a record-holder for the longest time spent thinking in Hell?"

"You remember Adam, the hermit who stood on one leg?"

"After all that piety, he went to Hell?"

"He lasted ten years in Hell. By the time he got to Heaven again, he had gained weight and the use of both of his legs."

"What's he doing in Heaven now, still playing board games?"

"Eventually he decided to be a Physical Fitness Trainer. He

helps small groups of women to exercise more, instead of just asking God to make them thinner and more attractive. So God lets them do their own thing, however they want to. Rather slender now, he looks and acts like a 20-year-old from the movies. By the way, the few statistics I just gave you about Hell are not lies. I got them directly from the Holy Spirit, who loves to deal with large numbers. And is also a whiz on computers. Best invention since the hand-held calculator, He says."

"What else should we see in Hell?"

"The usual things: the pictures of Hell that you've seen or had described to you—suffering bodies, Tantalus reaching for food or water which continues to move just out of his reach—all the ideas that you had on Earth about Hell can be seen in your visits here. Just like Heaven, Hell is what you think it is. At least, you can see what you imagined you would see. Then you begin to grow as you gain more information about Hell. You change your mind, your beliefs. In fact, the majority of Newcomers doesn't even bother to visit Hell. They find that Heaven is enough for them. Anything in Hell that you'd particularly like to see?"

"I don't think so. However, I do have a couple questions about Hell and how it works. Does anyone end up in Hell permanently?"

"Not so far. In extreme cases, such as Hitler and Stalin, God has assured them that His Grace has already blotted out all of their sins. Those two, and a few others like them, have insisted on being punished. God, in His spirit of Grace and Compromise, has required Stalin and Hitler to speak to each person whose death they were responsible for. Hitler and Stalin must ask forgiveness from each person, one at a time. With the hundreds of thousands, more probably millions, of persons whom they caused to die, God worked out a method of repentance. Each person whom they killed appears in the mind of Stalin or Hitler, gives his or her name, and then they ask each individual for forgiveness. With God in charge, all requests for forgiveness are accepted by each victim. At first, both men were only able to do this highly unique penance for a few hours at a time. Then they returned to Heaven to regain their strength and courage to ask for forgiveness from each individual whom they had sinned against. Later, they returned to Hell to face their accusers for days at a time before, in agony and despair, they returned to Heaven for God's help. Being separated from the love and joy of God was truly Hell for them. But God worked out this elaborate penance system so that each person could forgive himself. A compromise that God made worked again."

"So even God compromises at times?"

"All the time. That's what his limitless Grace is all about."

"And the occasional person who can't forgive himself?"

"It's never happened. God will keep working with each person until that person has accepted his Eternal Salvation."

"Have we talked enough about Hell? Should we move on?"

'We've probably talked too much about Hell. But do you feel that you now understand more clearly how God works?"

"I believe I do. Still some things require more thinking time."

"Just like the other Newcomers. That's why we Guides, whether talking to individuals or small groups, help you to accept Heaven as the wonder that it is and Hell as a place that simply isn't that interesting. What would you like to talk about next?"

"On Earth, we spent a lot of time thinking about sex. Some of us participated in sex more than others. Can we talk about sex?"

"O.K., but I should warn you that this part of our Heavenly discussions tends to run too long. I may call a halt to our questions and answers about sex. For me, sex discussion gets more boring each time I talk about it. Both your questions and my answers will tend to be repetitious."

'So you're not going to be like the teacher who turned to prostitution? She was a great favorite with all her customers because her motto was 'We're going to do this over and over and over, until we get it right!' "

"And now you've gotten rid of another one of your oft-repeated jokes. We'll never have to hear that one again."

"What one? I believe I've forgotten it already. Something about a teacher—so it must have been academic?"

"Yes, and a little far-fetched. Here in Heaven sex will be a little boring because, unlike Earth, where you must walk the walk, here in Heaven we're allowed just to 'talk the talk.' Ready for Amendment Five?"

"Yeah, sure, you betcha! (We used to say that a lot when we lived in Minnesota.)"

"I know, I know. But remind me, where else did you live?"

"Colorado—getting my M.A. from the U. of Colorado, and teaching at Trinidad State Jr. College for five years while I started work on my Ph.D. at the U. of Denver."

"But never anything useful, like engineering or mathematics. Ah! The look on your face was worth that cheap shot. I was just kidding, you know. I guess that folks who end up as college professors don't usually have much of a sense of humor."

"No, I guess I don't. Could we just get on with it, please?"

Chapter 7

The End of Sex
(OR "Who Cares?")

"Amendment Five: There is no sex in Heaven (either in thought or action). God tried permitting the Cave People to have sex, but it was just too noisy and created too many problems. God's decision for No Sex has been final for centuries and is not apt to be changed."

"And the noise factor was ...?"

"I'll let you remember, briefly, about your sexual activity on Earth. Was it ever noisy?"

"Well, being married for eight years before we had kids, I remember that their arrival did quiet love-making down some. Comments from most couples—yes, I know there are threesomes, even group sex, but—"

"Stop! Stop! You're not giving a lecture on all sexual possibilities. Just answer my noise question as briefly and as truthfully as you can. But briefly, briefly, please."

"O.K. Golly (that's not a bad word, is it?), you're hardly any fun at all. Can't you even talk about sex?"

"Go! Go!"

"All right! Yes, if things were going well, there were encouraging sounds. If things got even better, the sounds got louder and faster. In fact, a TV comedian—"

Roger groaned. "Another of your bad jokes?"

"But the bright side: If I tell a joke (good or bad) in Heaven, I will then forget it and never tell it again! Anyway, this comedian, surely an ironic agnostic, has suggested that God provided extra nerves on both female and male sex organs so that in reaching climax, shouts of 'God! God! God!' reminded the participants, and everyone else within earshot, that God was the prime mover in setting up the sexual responses that made human reproduction a certainty. Some people, usually very religious folks, gave up female-male sexual activity, except for reproduction. A majority of us found sex the most enjoyable recreational activity on Earth. A small minority preferred drag racing, golf, or parachuting, but—"

"Stop! Please stop!"

"But I've hardly begun!"

"I know, I know! But you're supposed to be learning about Heaven, not recalling your own Earthly experiences. Stop already."

"Sorry. Am I allowed to remember the murmurs, loving encouragement, even shouts of enjoyment during sex?"

"Now—can you imagine the additional enjoyment, excitement, and shouting that could occur in the heightened atmosphere of Heaven? The problem? Even joyous noise, if too loud and going on for too long, gets to be bothersome after a while. Especially if you're just a listener, not a participant."

"Any additional problems?"

"Yes. God didn't care about who slept with whom, but the Newcomer wives and husbands from Earth did care. Even with the Cave People, who were allowed one wife after the male was about 16 years old and had killed ten or more deer or a couple elk by himself and became a hero. Additional wives were allowed for more deer and elk, plus killing robbers from other tribes. So most Cave Men had at least two wives, many more if they were very strong, brave, and lucky in wars with neighbors. Huge mammoths were always attacked by a group. In fact, five young men, not older and experienced hunters, could each have a wife if they worked together to kill a woolly mammoth."

"Why was the mammoth killing so important?"

One Man's Heaven

"Because one adult mammoth could provide about 30 Cave People with meat for six months. And the meat could be preserved by drying in the sun, smoking and even salting (for those living close to a place where salt could be harvested). Cold and ice in the winter months also helped to preserve meat."

"You couldn't really cheat in this mammoth system to get more wives, could you?"

"Yes, one clever Cave Man noticed a small herd of mammoths grazing in tall grass in a meadow. Suddenly, a couple mammoths reared back in fear, trumpeted loudly, and led the group away from the grassy meadow. The Cave Man noticed this strange behavior, by different woolly mammoth herds, several times in the same grassy spot. He crept up close, looked over a nearby rise in the ground and saw some fairly large mouse-like animals, about the size of a small cat, eating grass, then running back and forth to their holes in the ground. That's what scared the mammoths. The Cave Man caught half a dozen of these rodents and put them in a cage made of deer ribs. Then the Cave Man carefully encouraged a wandering herd of mammoths close to the edge of a cliff bordering a river close by. Then he rushed the mammoth herd, waving his cage of the long-tailed varmints."

"And this worked? You're kidding!"

"No, it worked! Most of the mammoths escaped to the right or left, but in the confusion of butting and bellowing, one mammoth lost its balance on a grassy slope above the river, falling to its death 75 feet below. And the Cave Man's reward? Having killed a mammoth all by himself, the elders decided he could have five wives, as had been awarded to the regular number of five men usually needed to kill a mammoth."

"And they all lived happily ever after."

"The young Cave Man was advised to add only one wife at a time to his cave so they could work out a schedule of when each wife would sleep with him. Unfortunately, the young man became the victim of his own scheme. The first wife kept him pretty busy until he got her pregnant in a few weeks, cutting down her desire and availability. So he took a second wife who also kept him pretty busy, with the pregnant wife filling in the few blank spots. The young man took a third wife after his second wife got pregnant very quickly. But there were problems. The young man wasn't getting much work done, felt a little puny, and realized his sex drive had shifted into low gear. Not long after this, he died. The elders recognized their error and limited all men to no more than two wives. This is where adultery entered the picture, causing quarreling and many major fistfights."

"But why did God take away all sex in Heaven? I see no connection between the Cave People problems on Earth and no Heavenly sex."

"The turmoil over sex among the Cave People on Earth carried over to Heaven. What did a man do about having two Earthly wives when they got to Heaven? The wives thought that in the afterlife each woman would be able to have a man to herself. Monogamy had occurred to people on Earth, particularly women, but there was no chance for one husband/one wife until you got to Heaven. So there were disputes, loud quarrels, almost continuous arguing about sex, until, along with the excessive noise of love-making, God just had enough. No more sex, in thought or deed. God could eliminate all sexual thoughts and actions at once because He was God, the Almighty. Heaven would be the way He wanted it. The results were obvious at once— the noise level dropped to the quiet harp level, and all quarrels and fighting stopped."

"And God felt this major change about no sex in Heaven was worth the decision."

"Yes, and because they had no memory of sex, and all sexual thoughts and desires were gone, the residents of Heaven were happy, too. God has spoken: No more sex in Heaven! Amen!"

"What about another major concern of many conservative Christians against the abomination of gay sex?"

"Those Christians need to check their King James versions of the Bible for other abominations. Such as the abomination of not providing needed food and shelter for the widows and orphans in the world. We need to understand this as God's expected response from all of us for the poor and hungry on Earth."

"I didn't realize there were other abominations."

"Most Christians don't, but, after a brief review of Earthly abominations in my Guide training (remember: learning is faster and easier in Heaven), I can recall other abominations, offering children as human sacrifices, and having sex with a woman wearing a man's clothing or a man putting on women's clothing—or a proud look or a lying tongue. If it has to do with sex (especially if other people are doing it and they are not), some people in the United States get really upset, so gays are an easy target. The gays go to Hell and couldn't be members of their church. God isn't as interested in sex on Earth as many people think He is."

Roger went on: "In Europe, the general population seems less concerned about the gays than many Americans are. The Roman Catholic Church and some of the far right American Protestants are strange bedfellows (sorry about that play on words—no, I'm not!) on the gay question."

"We don't spend a lot of time in our Guide training on gayness, but we are told that about 10% of the American male population is gay. A majority of American adults believe that being gay is genetic—there is no choice involved. Many others, however, are certain that being gay is a learned behavior, a conscious choice. Some Americans have, however, recently agreed that what is acceptable for male/male sex is also all right for female/female. Quite a step for the male-dominated political system in the United States."

"And we are reminded of the ancient Greeks, who not only accepted close male bonding, including sex, but the army of Thebes even had an infantry unit made up entirely of paired male lovers. The concept behind this was that these men would fight harder than usual because each man was protecting the person whom he loved most. To most American citizens, this seems a very extreme recruiting method."

"Back to sex in Heaven. An additional logical reason for no sex is that no further propagation is needed in Heaven. Ironically, as the persons on Earth die, they provide the newest residents in Heaven."

I still had a question: "One of the biggest problems with sex on Earth today is that sexually transmitted diseases, particularly

AIDS, are weakening whole countries in Africa, mostly among the heterosexual members of the affected areas, who are dying by the thousands each week. As on Earth, we can still love, without sex, in Heaven?"

"You betcha! Without any concern whether lovers are male or female. God's overwhelming love is concerned only with changes, with growing up in Heaven to become the person God wants you to be."

Heaven kept sounding better and better. "Because you are in Heaven, you have the place and the time to change, to grow, to accept God's love?"

"So start enjoying Heaven while you're still on Earth. If God really loves you (and He does), you are a already saved for Heaven, not Hell. God's love is stronger than yours. Free Will is an interesting theory, but nothing is more powerful than God's will. Regardless of what *you* do on Earth (and because you accept God's love while you're on Earth, you will do good things for others), you will make life on Earth, better, not *perfect*. That's for Heaven."

"But beware of those on Earth who preach judgment, fear, and Hell rather than Heaven?"

"Exactly. Some people say you must believe this or must do that—or you'll go to Hell and be separated from God. And if someone tells you to hate not the sinner but the sin, just remember God's love, forgiveness, and unlimited Grace. These gifts of God not only assure you of your place in Heaven but make your Earthly life happier. Each of us should learn—and help others to learn—how to accept God's many gifts, including sex, on Earth."

Chapter 8

Our Family in Heaven
(OR "Not Exactly What You Had in Mind")

"Amendment Six: You may visit the members of your family who got to Heaven before you did. (Special permission is required if you visit them in Hell. Do not expect too much of your first visit, especially if you are Lutheran.) You will recognize one another easily, probably embrace and kiss (unless you are of Scandinavian descent). You will probably find that your family members have already made a smooth transition to Heaven and will feel much closer to God than to you."

I asked, "You said that at first Heaven will be pretty much what we expected it to be. Many Newcomers have great hopes of being joyously reunited with a particular family member. Perhaps a husband or a wife, father or mother, possibly a child who died young. Will that happen?"

"Yes, it will. And the more traditional Christians, for example, will enter the Pearly Gates and have St. Peter checking off their names in the Good Book. They will probably discover as they file through multiple Pearly Gates (no waiting!) that a sign above the checker may not read 'St. Peter,' but 'St. Peter's Assistant today is Pope John the XXIII' (or Martin Luther, John Wesley, Billy Graham, etc.). This is organized so that Catholics will pass through the Pope's gate, Lutherans and associates by

Luther, Methodists by Wesley, and most born again Christians by Graham."

"Is it considered a great honor to be a substitute Gatekeeper? Who makes the choice? Is that the only job that the Pope and Luther have in Heaven?"

"Yes, it is a great honor to take a turn as an Assistant Gatekeeper. You help the traditional Newcomers to feel 'Wow! This really is Heaven! Look, my name's being checked off and read aloud. What a blast!' Of course, the whole entering system has been simplified. In the Old Days, when there were fewer people in the World, the Gatekeeper read aloud the Good Deeds that each person had done on Earth. Even then, there were no Bad Deeds because the unconditional Grace of God had blotted out all the sins.

"You were just talking about the Christian Holy Gates, right? Because I'm a Christian."

"Right. The Jews, Moslems, Hindus, Buddhists, and others have entrances that look different. But their Gatekeepers are their religious leaders, or even their gods."

"I suppose that all Gates are open 24/7, so there must be a host of Gatekeepers?"

"Indeed, there are. And God has all that information on computers so the Assistant Gatekeepers are reminded of their times to be on the job. And the rules are fairly strict: each Assistant Gatekeeper may serve for only one 24-hour time period during every 100 Earth Days. St. Peter, of course, may serve as often as he likes. He is more than repaid for his time and effort by the awe, wonder, and great joy that is shown on the faces and felt in the hearts of the Newcomers as they are allowed to pass through his gate. Many even shout, 'Amen! Amen!' as they pass by. Most of the Lutherans just pinch themselves and murmur, 'It's really true! I'm in! Thank you, God!' "

"This duty is made easier by the fact that these leaders no longer feel hunger, plus needing no rest or sleep, right?"

"Correct. Incidentally, a few Assistant Gatekeepers are allowed to pull a double shift (48 continuous hours) every 100 days. Mother Teresa is one of these Saints. She just loves being a Gatekeeper, even switching over to some of the non-Christian Gates. As she served the poor most of her life in India, members of the Hindu and Buddhist faiths knew her there and loved her and her work."

"Are there any popular modern preachers who might not be chosen by God to be a Gatekeeper?"

"Yes, it's been rumored that folks like Pat Robertson would probably have to wait around for a century or two before they could qualify. Generally, religious leaders on Earth who preach fear, hatred, and even violence rather than the Love, Grace, and Forgiveness of God are not chosen to be Gatekeepers. Those Moslem leaders who encourage their followers to terrify and even kill in the name of religion are not interpreting the Love of God correctly as He speaks to them in the Koran. Just like those Christians who demand the death of doctors who perform legal abortions."

"Enough of this heavy stuff. Let's find out about the Joy of being united with family members. What should we expect? What should we do?"

"Heaven begins as a place that we expect it to be. In the past, Hell on Earth began when someone very close to us—a wife, a husband, or a child—died. Left grieving for our loss, we complained about life on Earth and prayed for the day when our reunion with that person would make a perfect Heaven for us. It probably won't turn out exactly that way. But God is willing to compromise with us about what Heaven should be. The Joy of Heaven is being with God, growing in the knowledge and acceptance of God's Will, changing to fit God's Heaven as He planned it for us. Our love and attachment for a family member with whom we are reunited will grow stronger, but God will still have first place in our hearts. We can change our beliefs and attitudes, making Heaven perfect."

"You surely give long answers. Are you sure that you weren't a college professor on Earth? I almost feel tongue-tied compared to you, Roger."

"I'm only doing my job: helping you understand Heaven better, and to accept God's Love and Grace more completely.

God is bigger, smarter, more imaginative than we can ever be. Heaven is the happiest place for us to spend Eternity. Nothing else can begin to compare."

"Any other comments or suggestions on our family in Heaven?"

"I'll try for a final comment—but you'll probably try to lead me astray—again! You'll have a new family in Heaven. Like Earth in some ways, your family in Heaven will grow in size, in relationships, in what you can do, and with whom. You'll be working at various jobs until you find the particular task that you like to do best. By accepting this assignment, you will show your love to God as well as the others in your growing family. Your new knowledge, your improved attitude, and the new people with whom you work will make you a better person. Accept changes, look for changes, and use changes to help you grow in your love for God and for the other Newcomers in your Heavenly life."

"Sounds almost scary! Do you think that I can do it?"

"You'll do more than just do it! You'll help others so that their lives in Heaven will be all that they can be. All of this will be possible with the limitless Grace of God.

"Wow! I hope so."

"God has it waiting for you. And it will be better than you can imagine."

Chapter 9

Worshipping God
(OR "Just Do It!")

"Amendment Seven: You will quickly learn that whatever you do in Heaven is a means of worshipping God and serving your fellow Newcomers. No special churches or altars or rituals are used. But, yes, there are helpful Angels—most of them with harps—who will assist you if you have any questions or need advice about proper methods of worship."
 "Speaking of Angels, how come I haven't seen any so far?"
 "Guess. You'll figure it out if you just think about it."
 "Oh, yeah—I wasn't too sure there *were* Angels in Heaven. I'm more easily convinced now. Does that mean I'll probably see an Angel after I've talked about them for awhile?"
 "Yup! Look over there to your right, off in the distance but headed our way."
 "Wow! And it's one of those super jobs with three sets of wings. A seraph?"
 "You got it!"
 "I often wondered how they used those wings. This one seems to be flying with the pair on his back, crossing a second pair in front of his face, while the third pair covers his feet. Can an Angel—? Wow! Look at that! "The Angel used all three

Eugene Jacobson

sets of wings to speed up and zipped by us in a couple seconds. Soon the seraph was a speck in the distance to my left.

"Did you get the feeling that Angel was showing off a bit?"

"Did you see how he grinned at us as he rocketed by? I had no idea that Heavenly Angels were allowed to have a sense of humor. Another new idea about Heaven."

Roger laughed at the surprise and shock that showed clearly on my face. "Angels bring tidings of great joy to people on Earth."

"Not only are they Good News messengers, but they don't play tricks on Earth or in Heaven. They're like good cops on Earth. If anyone on Earth needs help or a quick answer to a difficult question, just thinking about it will bring an Angel (or two—they usually travel in pairs. I don't know why.)."

"Are two Angels in an emergency better than one?"

"Probably. They have the solution every time. Sort of God's handy helpers."

"Are there female as well as male Angels?"

"Yes. They even tend to look alike, so expect a combination of both male and female facial features, but with a great individuality among them. Each is very different from all the others—you'll never forget one of their faces and, this being Heaven, you'll never forget their names. Another oddity for Newcomers is that every Angel has a different name from every other Angel. Yes, there is a Tom, a Mary, a Henry, a Lyla, but only one of each in Heaven."

"And there are thousands of Angels in Heaven (and on Earth?) Don't they run out of names?"

"Surprisingly, there are a total of only about 20,000 Angels. Approximately 2,000 Angels in each of the ten classes. I say approximately as God isn't as tied to round numbers as we are on Earth. There are probably a few hundred extra Angels in each of the ten types."

"Don't Angels wear out? Get to retire? Choose another work for Eternity?"

"Nope. They just keep doing their thing, ever since God created them fairly early in the history of Heaven. The Cave People didn't pile up in large numbers, so God was able to handle them alone (being three persons in one came in handy, too). But God added St. Peter early on. By the way, the Peter in Christ's time was not the original Peter, who was a decidedly earlier Peter who left his life on Earth to become the famous St. Peter of Heaven. Before long, God created the Angels, too, and eventually turned over the everyday Heavenly details entirely to their care."

"How did the Angels manage to care for the Heavenly Newcomers when the numbers began to run into the thousands per day?"

"At first, God just created more Angels as needed, but with the help of modern machines, such as computers, fewer Angels were needed. Then, too, God decided that every Newcomer would also work half-time to help meet the needs of Heaven."

"Hey, I'm beginning to see more Angels! Many different sizes, plus hair which is brunette, blond, or red, just like Earth. And I'm seeing more Angels because…?"

"Because you believe in them now, more and more all the time. So God lets you see another part of Heaven more clearly, now that you believe."

"I expected Angels to wear haloes, too. Or are haloes limited to the Big Three and other dignitaries?"

"Angels have haloes that are flexible. Not too big to begin with, when taken from the head they shrink so that they fit into the Angel's robe pocket. Because they travel around so fast (you're not ready yet to be told how fast), the haloes are usually pocketed and saved for more formal occasions like the entrance of an important Saint, such as Mother Teresa, or an annual Holy Hymn Sing."

"The haloes are either silver or gold?"

"Yes, and all the Angels in a particular order (seraphim, cherubim, etc.) wear the same color, either gold or silver."

"Is there any reason why all of the same class wear either gold or silver?"

"Tradition! Tradition!"

"Oh, my! Even in Heaven!"

"We like to have things like rituals and haloes stay the same. Over and over. God likes change more than most of us. Just to keep us on our toes, He changes something almost every year. He doesn't care for *always* or *never*. God likes variety and change, so get used to it."

"Enough about Angels and Heavenly changes! We're supposed to be discussing what?"

"How everything we do in Heaven is worshipping God. Even my providing Heavenly information to you and your listening to me and trying to understand what I say. Both of these kinds of work are done for the Glory of God."

"I'll have to think about that for awhile. Your meaning is clear, but I'm still sort of attached to my past beliefs about worship: attending church, kneeling, even bowing my head. Do most Newcomers accept their daily activities as a proper way to worship God?"

"Some Newcomers have a hard time giving up their traditional religious practices, such as certain kinds of prayer, particular types of leaders or liturgy and hymns. God allows them a transitional period for them to continue their usual Earthly worship customs."

"Does the transition take a long time?"

"Changes take place rather quickly in Heaven. For instance, very few Newcomers (regardless of the country on Earth that they come from or their Earthly religion), need to sleep at all after they've been in Heaven a week or two, at the most. If they feel the need to eat at all, this desire disappears in a few days. It begins to dawn on most of them that many changes will need to be made in Heaven. Differences between people and how they worship are not only expected but accepted. With no rain, no wind, no blazing sun, if you still worship in a group, you can do it outside, in the open air. Gradually, the Newcomers accept their daily activities in Heaven as ways of worshipping God."

"Doesn't this cause some problems?"

"Remember: this is Heaven. One person is not trying to get another one to change his beliefs. A kindly God is in charge. And everyone feels happy, so glad to be in Heaven, where God has written the rules for entering Heaven. For Eternal Salvation, the only question in the Newcomer's mind becomes 'How can

I worship God and serve my neighbors from Earth (all people) in Heaven.'"

"Isn't all that pretty complicated for some Newcomers?"

"How? Give me an example."

"I have to include a little bit of humor to make my point ..."

"Praise God that once you've told your stories in Heaven, no one will ever have to hear you repeat them again! Get it over with."

"You know, Heaven really is a wonderful place. Back on Earth, I would have been irritated, probably angry, maybe even swearing a little after your critical comments. Instead, now I just take your well-meaning criticism as another method for teaching me the ways of God in Heaven."

"Please, please! Just tell the story."

O.K. I'll even cut it down, so I'll get to the point sooner."

"Please do—now!" Roger murmured, "Thank you, God, for making me serve as a Guide to only a few professors. They are good-hearted but too long-winded."

After a long-winded pause, I continued, "After asking how many Presbyterians, Methodists, Catholics, and others it takes to change a light bulb, the same question was asked of a group of Lutherans. In chorus, they replied, 'Change?!' "

"And you never get to repeat that story again. God makes good rules."

"And where were we?"

"I don't even know anymore."

"Ah, yes! Do Lutherans sometimes have a little trouble adjusting to Heaven?"

"Almost always. But you usually fit in pretty well in a week or two. A few of them can't accept the Universal Salvation Amendment immediately and go to Hell, but all of them return to Heaven soon. The majority of them in a few days or weeks, but the really tough nuts may take a couple of years."

"But back to our discussion, how does God give Newcomers, from all religions and all parts of the world time to adjust their religious activities to Heaven?"

Eugene Jacobson

"You might think that it would be difficult for Muslims to change their prayer ritual (five times a day, shoes off, kneeling on a rug, facing Mecca), but God just told them which way was East, so they all prayed in that direction. Surprisingly, after a week or two of the Joys of Heaven, most Muslims accepted the idea of worshipping God by their daily work in Heaven."

"God is good. With good rules."

"I should also mention again that Guides not only teach individuals but also groups. People with close ethnic or religious ties may be assigned in groups of 100 individuals who escort them on a tour of Heaven, going over the 10 Amendments and reminding the Newcomers that they no longer have to eat or sleep. Some Newcomers make the no eating-sleeping adjustment within a day or two. Others find snacks of their favorite candy bars in the pockets of their robes. Miraculous! If either bar is eaten, a new one takes its place. Any candy bars removed from the robe pockets, even when put in a safe place (a cool spot under a tree) spoil within half an hour. All of these changes help the Newcomer to adjust to the changes of Heaven. Soon everyone reacts positively to the 24/7 life of Heaven."

"Any final advice about how to worship God properly in Heaven?"

"Just a reminder that *whatever we do in Heaven*—guiding, learning, playing everything from touch football to a harp, our main work—all our Heavenly efforts are ways of worshipping God."

"If I do think of a question about this later, I can always ask, right?"

"Right—there are no restrictions on what you ask or when you ask it."

"So—onward and upward! (That doesn't work so well in Heaven, does it?)"

Chapter 10

Everybody Goes to Heaven (OR "No! That Can't Be!")

"Amendment Eight - All people go to Heaven when they die (Universal Salvation). This idea is not accepted by all Newcomers when they first enter Heaven. We need to remember: God makes the rules here. With all the varying Earthly ideas about Heaven which the Newcomers bring with them, at first there are many Heavens. God allows all Newcomers to find Heaven as they imagined it. Gradually, they learn to accept God's Heaven. And the Real Thing is much better."

"Why is it so difficult for Newcomers to accept the idea that God's Grace can forgive all sins for everybody? If that is what God wants to do, it will be done."

"Most Christian Newcomers have no trouble accepting God as all-powerful. However, many of those same Christians can't believe that God would forgive everyone. Not Hitler and Stalin, as we've mentioned. Plus plenty of other people whom you have met on Earth— surely, they don't deserve Heaven! They lied to you, failed to respect you, or made a pass at your wife or husband, etc."

Roger went on: "We've made so many rules about unacceptable human behavior. We forget that God made adultery a sin because it begins with cheating, then leads to lying, often to divorce (and the breakup of families) or even physical violence and death. God was trying to spare us from some of the problems of Earth by having us avoid those actions which may lead to sinful behavior, which causes great pain to both ourselves and those we love."

"Will I understand all this? Am I smart enough, open enough, ready to learn?"

"You'll do just fine. Here's a story that will help: God took a long time to create the world and its creatures, including us. He made mistakes; some of them he corrected. This was God's first creative urge; He had never created on this scale before. Not only everything on Earth but also throughout all space. From countless stars to countless universes. But God always had a particular fondness for Earth, especially its human inhabitants. He created Mankind so that they could change over time, a process that we now call Evolution."

"Many people on Earth still do not accept the idea of Evolution. But you tell me it's true."

"They'll believe in it once they get to Heaven—and they *will* get here. God had some problems in creating Earth, however. Having a liquid core in the Earth helped its stability as it spun around the Sun, even making Earth's gravity work better than if Earth had a solid core. But God had a little trouble with volcanoes on Earth as they connected with their hot liquid core. God never quite got the volcanoes under control; they continued pouring out smoke, rocks, and liquid lava, causing death and destruction for nearby villages and cities. Much the same problem came up from the shifting continental plates, causing earthquakes. Despite the ruined houses, bridges, and cities, God decided to let Nature take its course, ignoring the occasionally severe jolts to those who lived near the faults in the Earth's surface."

"But what about Universal Salvation?"

"You understand that most Newcomers to Heaven just accept God's Will on Eternal Rewards. Some of the Newcomers, however, got so upset that they took a visit to Hell as a type of protest against God's Grace to *all Mankind*. These Newcomers, because of what their parents taught them, perhaps even from

One Man's Heaven

what their religious leaders taught them, could not believe that any of Those People made it to Heaven. Those folks should be kept out of Heaven because of their skin color, religion, lack of education, etc. Mostly, just because they were so different from the Newcomers who had their own firmly held beliefs about Right and Wrong (usually merely Earthly prejudices) that they even dared to challenge God's saving Grace. God, of course, just waits. It may take several trips to Hell before the holier-than-thou Newcomers manage to accept all the 10 Amendments that God gives to Man. Especially Universal Salvation. God waits, patiently. The years roll by in minutes, even seconds, with the Joy of Heaven softening human hearts and freeing everyone to enjoy the comfort of Heaven. When most Newcomers first arrive, they see the variety of religious robes and native dress, decide quickly that God has open arms for all people, never mind their differences. A majority don their Heavenly Robes at once when they enter Heaven and accept the 10 Amendments. But some Newcomers take years before they can wear the Heavenly Robe. God encourages change in the Newcomers' lives. They become kinder, more loving, and more helpful to other Newcomers in their new Heavenly Home, leading to acceptance of Universal Salvation as the key to acceptance of and growth in the Heavenly Kingdom."

"But I still wonder how much difference the Earthly acceptance of Universal Salvation would have made on Earth. Would we have had the Christian Crusades against the Moslems? The Northern Ireland Protestants against all the Irish Catholics? Or all the wars and genocide in the world when people fail to see the likenesses rather than the differences between themselves and their Neighbors, whom they should protect and feed rather than kill and starve. Maybe then we might have had Peace in the world?"

"Perhaps just the acceptance of the possibility of Peace on Earth, strengthened by an overpowering belief in Universal Salvation, might someday be accepted on Earth. With God's help and encouragement."

"God still controls the Good that happens on Earth?"

"Of course. He controls the Good by using the hearts and

minds of Good People on Earth. Those who already know the Joys of Heaven, even as they must still have their struggles on Earth. God will help them on Earth as He helps us in Heaven."

"Now all we have to do is to use our increased Love of God to include our Neighbors, who are all the Peoples in the world."

"But that's a lot! Perhaps, if we give God our help while we are still on Earth, God may make it happen: Peace on Earth."

"Amen! Let it be so!" I agreed.

"Now—are you ready to explore your choices among the possibilities for Heavenly Activities?

"Yup—let's do it!"

Chapter 11

Finding My Place
(OR "Then You Did It; Now You Don't!")

"Amendment Nine: Feel free to try as many Heavenly experiences and activities as you like. Your goal is to decide how you will worship God and serve your Neighbors in Heaven—for Eternity. No rush: you may make changes in your plans at any time, with no limit on the number of changes that you make. With Eternity, you have plenty of Time."

"I have no idea how to begin. Any suggestions?"

"Several. First of all, what was your favorite recreational activity?"

"Reading. After I retired, particularly biography. But also modern fiction—novels and short stories."

"A remarkably good choice for Heaven. I suggest that you start with the works that you planned to read on Earth, but you never got around to. Despite the fact that you will read at least twice as fast as you did on Earth—and remember more than you did there (but not everything—that's God's special ability). It usually takes about ten years or so of Eternity for you to play catch-up."

"How can that be? All the published material in English alone should take me ten years!"

"You just noted how your thinking is too narrow. God has made many skills either easily learned or unnecessary in Heaven.

One big difference here is that there is no longer such a thing as a foreign language. Whether written or spoken, all words are instantly understood by all readers and listeners. In your case, all words are immediately understood by you in English."

"Has God set up special computers that translate all these words? It sounds impossible, like magic."

"Or a miracle? What makes you think that God can only do miracles on Earth? You will see many miracles during your Eternity in Heaven. Most of them will surprise you; some will even shock you. For instance, you're still having trouble believing that not only Stalin but also Hitler have made it to Heaven. To you it seems neither fair nor logical that both of them should be here?"

"You're correct. It just doesn't seem right!"

"But you forgot that God is in charge in Heaven. And God changes things, especially people."

"And Hitler and Stalin have been changed to…?"

"To kind, loving people. You will see the change. Hitler loves to work with babies and young people. Remember, it took many years and over a dozen trips to Hell before he accepted his place in Heaven. Until Hitler started it, no one took the Newcomers to see the different parts of Heaven. Until then, many Heavenly residents didn't know that there were mountains, oceans, even deserts in Heaven. In the pre-Hitler eras, God simply placed Newcomers in geographical areas like the places where they lived on Earth. When their home country consisted mainly of mountains, many Newcomers thought all of Heaven was mountainous. But when Hitler made up his mind to settle in Heaven, God still didn't have regular tours to all parts of Heaven. With God's permission, Hitler got to try out his tour idea. At first, Hitler's tours covered the most recognized parts of Heaven, including the Heavenly Gate (with St. Peter as Head Man), the Royal Throne area with Father, Son, and Holy Spirit all seated formally, and parts of the Golden Road. All of this took careful planning to have everyone in place, but God helped iron out the problems. All tours took three Earth days in the beginning, and at no time was any Newcomer forced to go on

One Man's Heaven

the tour. In fact, only about half of the Newcomers were willing to spend any time on an activity which took the place of the Work for Eternity which the Newcomers would choose. Now, about 75% of all Newcomers take the tour, with the numbers inching up, decade by decade."

"I can't imagine any Newcomers not wanting to tour all of Heaven as soon as possible after they arrive."

"Of course you couldn't! Folks like priests/pastors, college professors, and (surprise?) politicians couldn't get enough of the tours. Newcomers like you folks, plus a sprinkling of those with unusually inquisitive minds, not only enjoyed the traveling and the looking, but also started taking notes about what they saw."

"What's so unusual about that? How can we remember what we see if we don't have notes to help us?"

"Here in Heaven you understand more quickly and remember more exactly than you did on Earth. Secondly, God didn't care if those Newcomers took notes, even in Heaven. But some adjustments had to be made. Just as their taking notes took too long."

"And the Politicians? I'm a little surprised they're note-takers. Was there a special problem with politicians in Heaven just as there is on Earth?"

"Yep. Politicians needed notes because of all the people they met. Assistants took careful notes of all the names of important people their bosses met at conventions, speaking engagements, political rallies, etc. Usually, the assistants were smart enough and skilled enough to avoid the usual order, 'Make a note of that!' Which meant in most cases the question or request to the politicians should be answered by a letter, an e-mail, or even a telephone call within the next 48 hours. But here in Heaven, the politicians no longer had assistants to take notes; the problem was that each politician had to do some remedial work on note-taking."

"How did this work for the politicians? Weren't they quick learners?"

"Our usual prejudice about politicians is that they're not very intelligent, just clever and sneaky. With some exceptions for local Politicians in some places on Earth, they are pretty bright and, like most of us, if there is something to be gained by learning how to use it, we understand and remember very quickly. God had his appropriate workers develop a Remedial Note-Taking #1 Course. Typically, a short course would take about three days, with individual help as needed beyond that. Rather unexpectedly, the best teachers in this course (a great variety of vocational backgrounds were represented in those selected and trained for this job) turned out to be the Angels, particularly the seraphim and cherubim."

"Any idea why this was so successful for the Angels?"

"In Heaven, we not only have an idea about why this is so, we know. As a part of their work on Earth, Angels have a number of people to keep track of and help. In the Old Days, they used to take notes by writing on paper (or something as useful), returning the notes to St. Peter and his associates. Permanent record of these notes was kept for ten years, then destroyed. Nowadays, the Angels use computers, with either e-mail or voice mail, for reporting all they have observed about their clients and how the Angels helped the Earth People with their problems. Simpler. Faster. Less paper."

"But I sense another problem with the Newcomer note-takers."

"There was another. Hitler worked out a variety of tour lengths, depending on who the Newcomers were. A majority of the Newcomers get a one-day (24 hours—no need for eating or sleeping) whirlwind tour of all the parts of Heaven, explaining not only what is seen but how it is useful in Heaven. There is little or no note-taking, so each Newcomer receives a booklet of about 200 pages, fully illustrated, in color. For most people the one-day tour suits them just fine."

"It's the politicians, clergy members, professors—the note-takers—who are a problem?"

"Actually, not too big a problem. To begin with, only about 25% of the Newcomers want a longer tour. And God saw no problem with that. So Hitler set up a 7-day tour, with time allowed for rather brief discussions at each major stopping place. Again, with no need for food or sleep (and allowing an exception to the daily 50% Work/50% Recreation Rule) an amazing number of sights and sounds, and their use in Heaven, can be covered. In addition a 500-page paperback, with a complete index and numerous color illustrations, served as a handy reference.

"So much for Hitler's Heavenly Tours."

"Not quite. One more refinement. For the Newcomers who liked the tour very much, special classes were set up. These tour lovers were allowed to do research about their favorite parts of Heaven and to act as stopping point assistants to the regular Guides who led Heavenly tours. These Tour Specialists constantly update tour booklets and paperbacks, and help set up computer programs to evaluate the Heavenly Tours. Ninety-seven percent of the Newcomers who take the tour felt that it was a part of Eternity well-spent, so even in Heaven things don't always work 100%. But God was pleased and continues to support the tour program. Some of those who received the advanced classes became full-time Heavenly Tour Guides. So that job became their Heavenly Work for as long as they wanted to continue guiding. The turnover rate was nearly 75% over five decades. Pretty high, but God was pleased and so were the Guides."

"So Hitler started the Heavenly Tour, probably acted as the first Guide for the tour, and continues in the program now?"

"Hitler is still active. He's a sort of Professor Emeritus—he's encouraged to Guide occasional tours, but he's not regularly scheduled. It's at his request that he Guides, usually at least a half a dozen times a year."

"How are the Heavenly Tours organized? How many Newcomers are in each tour group? Are the tours available to Newcomers of the past centuries?"

"Again, this gets a little involved. It was Hitler's decision that groups should be of 25, individuals, preferably persons who knew one another on Earth. Or at least lived in the same country. The size of 25 per group has been kept, but there are some consequences to that decision. First of all, tours of Heaven are going on almost constantly (except during rare All-Heaven celebrations or when some particular area of Heaven is having an All-Area celebration). Now there about 1000 Heavenly Tour Guides. They must be allowed time off and vacations, so their schedules vary. Modern computers, souped up to Heaven-speed, keep fairly up-to-date with new arrivals, but pre-Hitler Newcomers are also allowed to go on Heavenly Tours. Only one tour per individual—updates on Heavenly changes are sent regularly to past visitors. So far, with a schedule working backward to pick up the Oldtimers on a space-available basis, the tours are caught up to about 1850. Because there were fewer people on Earth in previous times, the backlog should be complete in about 100 years."

"Pretty interesting, but shouldn't we get back on the track? How am I going to fit into this new Heaven?"

"By taking classes or workshops which will tie in with your past interests. Or some new areas you'd like to explore. With our large population, we can come up with a class or a workshop for a small group (20 or so) or even with your own tutor. These new sources of information are valuable not only to you as a learner, but also in case you choose to teach your own class, based on skills and ideas you already have, to other Newcomers."

I felt like I was getting it: "And as we learn new ideas and sharpen our skills, we also use what we've learned. That's the Eternal Work side of what we do. But 50% of our time is to be spent in Recreation?"

"Recreation is a pretty wide-open term in Heaven. While your Work has some useful purpose in Heaven, serving both to worship God and to help your fellow Heavenly Newcomers, your Recreation is something which you like to do. But if you're happy doing these things (usually a variety of activities), your joy will make both God and other Newcomers happy, too. You may choose to golf, play poker or chess, checkers, or Scrabble, or to garden, paint pictures, make pottery—anything you've always wanted to do. God doesn't care about your Recreation and Life Work, except that they contrast with one another. What

One Man's Heaven

you should be doing is growing in knowledge, understanding, and love so that you become a better person in Heaven. This process of changing, becoming better, is Eternal. God wants it to continue, so it will."

"But I can begin very simply on my Eternal Life Work just by reading books that I never got to on Earth?"

"Yes, that's a good first step for you. One of the main purposes of Heavenly Guides is to get you started on your Work. But we also want you to start your Recreation activities. Maybe you'd like to improve your golf game. God doesn't work miracles as you golf, but your improved learning skills and better memory help you get rid of that slight hook or slice that you never quite got corrected on Earth. The other Newcomers who golf with you will also be improving, so your game is less apt to include swearing and yelling as on Earth and more likely to bring smiles to all of your player-buddies. God helps you change, but improvement in golf still depends on concentration and lots of practice, even in Heaven."

"Would I be allowed to work with Shakespeare on one of his plays?"

"Yes, you would. There's a waiting list, of course, but it's not nearly as long as those who want Arnold Palmer as a golfing partner. Incidentally, Shakespeare writes new plays, too, even acting in them occasionally."

"Could I be in a play with Shakespeare, work beside him as an actor?"

"Yes, you could. And he's very kind, very talkative, and ready to share many of his ideas about playwriting. However, as I said before, there's a long waiting list. But this is Heaven; you'll be so busy, so happy, that it won't seem long at all! I should tell you something else—you know that Angels fly?"

"Yes, I've even seen one do it very fast! Remember?"

"You can learn to fly, too."

"I can fly? How? How soon? Is it dangerous?"

"It's not dangerous. Just don't get too excited—you'll scare the Lutherans. You'll learn how to fly by being carefully taught. And as you're not an exercise buff, it will take a while. But this is Heaven. All things are possible."

"Yippee! I can fly!"

"In the future, in the future. Calm down! You're supposed to be changing gradually. You were too excitable on Earth, but you can cool down a little now."

"Gotcha! I'll try. But Heaven is so exciting! Remind me again about how God instantly translates every language."

"You got that partly right. If you understand the foreign words, the original will not be translated."

"Oh, you mean like my Dad's 'Satan Hellveta!' when things weren't going well on our farm. That was Swedish for 'Devil, go to Hell,' a pretty mild oath, but it meant that it was best to shut up and help Dad get the pig back in its pen or the cow into the barn. By the way, how come I was allowed to say Hell?"

"Because you weren't cursing, just translating. I also need to remind you that because everything is easier and better in Heaven, writers improve in Heaven. Shakespeare has now written so many new sonnets, always improving, that many other writers are taking classes from him. He's such a good teacher: kind, helpful, supportive. He's more famous in Heaven than he ever was on Earth."

"I don't remember a Lutheran pastor ever mentioning such a possibility in Heaven."

"The idea probably never occurred to them."

"I'm still concerned about getting started on my Eternal Life Work in Heaven."

"Don't worry about it. A number of the Angels are especially trained to help Newcomers get started."

"What about Stalin? What did he end up doing?"

"Stalin took quite a few years and numerous trips to Hell before he finally decided. What he liked to do most of all on Earth was to play poker. (Poker in Heaven uses only chips, no money.) Stalin was particularly good at numbers, keeping exact count of all the cards played, then figuring out what his chances were to get a full house, an inside straight, etc. His goal is to teach all of his students so well that they can beat him at his own game of poker. It seems to be working. He's a wonderful teacher, very personal with his students, repeating techniques for judging the value of their chances, learning to cover the fact that they're bluffing. Most of his students use poker as part of their required Recreation. But Stalin is also studying the French Impressionist Movement—the artists, their famous paintings, techniques of painting, and their relative success on Earth as painters. Stalin plans to become a part-time Guide at the Heavenly Impressionist Art Museum. Lately, he's branched out to study Picasso, all of his painting periods and his theories about art."

"Who've been the most successful students in Stalin's poker classes?"

"He was almost as surprised as the rest of us were when the best poker players turned out to be Chinese women. They were very good listeners, very good at understanding and applying techniques taught them by Stalin, and were patient in their playing. These women were clearly more intelligent than any other group."

"Whatever happened to all the usual characteristics of a good poker party—the smoke-filled room, the beer, pretzels and potato chips, and the rough language that goes with the card playing?"

"All changed drastically—the games are played outdoors where a light breeze provides some of the perfumes of the flowers in Heaven. Everyone plays hard, enjoying the excitement, but always talking quietly with one another as they play and drink their tea. Incidentally, all Heavenly poker players use poker chips, but the winner each time can only buy Heavenly Perfume if female and Heavenly Aftershave if male. The variety of fragrances is in the thousands, but Chanel #5 for women and Old Spice for men are most popular. For the Chinese women, as poker players in God's Heavenly Presence, they are happier than they have ever been before."

"Don't all Newcomers feel that Heaven is really great, better than they'd ever expected?"

"No, some of them wanted more worship services like the ones they had on Earth. Or that the Trinity should only appear in Heaven as one God, not break into separate identities of the Father, Son, and Holy Spirit, which is the only way the Three-in-One ever appear in Heaven—as three distinct Gods. This makes the Absolute Monotheists pretty upset. By the way, if some Newcomers, such as Moslems or Jews, look at God directly (shielding your eyes may be necessary at times), they only see one God, until they get to meet enough Newcomers from other religions. Then it becomes no big deal in Heaven to see the Big Three separately. But some of the hard line Newcomers of all beliefs have to spend extra time in Hell (days, weeks, even years) before they finally accept Heaven as God made it."

"I'm still a little concerned about this Work/Recreation schedule in Heaven. Most of us Newcomers from Earth are conditioned to accept eight hours of work (usually more hours in poorer countries), then time to relax, eat, and sleep each day. With eating and sleeping no longer necessary for most us Newcomers in Heaven, how can we adjust to the 50/50 routine of God's Heaven? Can we make these changes easily?"

"Of course. Why are you so surprised? Don't you believe that God is smart enough and powerful enough so that He can solve all Heavenly problems through His Love and Grace. Especially with the help of His Angels."

"Oh, yeah. I keep forgetting. Sorry."

"That's O.K. That's why this one-on-one discussion is set up for hard cases. Oops!"

"So I'm a hard case? Why do you say that? You've shaken me up a bit."

"Sorry. All that I mean is that as a professor, you're used to being in charge. At least in your classroom, if not at home. You spend a lot of your time studying, thinking about and organizing the material that you teach. You try to be logical and truthful in what you present. You are seldom questioned or challenged to change your mind. Students know who decides on their final grades in the course and don't want to upset you. You know that you and the overwhelming majority of teachers with whom you have taught with make a conscious effort to avoid letting their own prejudices and beliefs affect their grading."

One Man's Heaven

"I still don't feel any closer to beginning my training for my Eternal Life's Work."

"I think you are. Your interest in literature and biography suggests that you want some more Newcomers to understand more clearly and enjoy more fully those kinds of writing."

"Wow! You mean that I could go on teaching for Eternity?"

"That's a strong possibility. And you could compare notes with Shakespeare, Chekhov, Shaw, Eugene O'Neill and the rest of the great writers to find out about certain unclear meanings in their plays and stories. But you will also remind the Newcomer of the adage: 'Once it's written and printed, the writing no longer belongs just to the author.' Later interpretations of the works are not only possible but often add to the multiple meanings in good creative literature. The reader can't simply say, 'It means whatever I say it means,' but the opinions of later readers can often add to the meanings which the original writer may have had in mind."

"Are you sure you've never taught literature?"

"Quite sure. On Earth I was a bookkeeper. Had to stick to facts and figures. But I read quite a bit. Not only novels and plays from my own period (early 1900's and on), but also the more poetic works of Shakespeare and English translations of Dante, Goethe, Socrates, and the more modern Ibsen and Strindberg. I had a wife, four children and a comfortable life—until I was killed in a train accident almost a hundred years ago. So I've been a Guide quite a while. And I like it. Oops! I gave you more than you wanted!"

"No need to apologize. I'm glad to know more about you. But do you think I *could* be a teacher in Heaven."

"Yes. Remember, too, that you can still change at any time. What about the other 50% of your time? Your Recreation."

"I believe I'd like to continue one of my hobbies on Earth. Gardening. Could I get my hands in real dirt, see plants and flowers grow and mature without God stepping in with some miracle or other?"

"Sure. That would give you a better chance of meeting Hitler, too, if you want to."

"Yes, I would. Mostly curiosity. How's this man who caused

so much Hell on Earth doing now that he's in Heaven?"

"He'd doing fine. Because he's right with God and with himself and other Newcomers to Heaven. He's happy and Heaven is happy with him. Only by the Grace of God could this happen."

"Amen! So I've made my choices for beginning Eternity: teaching literature (and classes in which I learn will more about my specialties, plus better techniques for teaching) and Recreation time that will begin with classes and hands-on experience in gardening."

"And Amen to that. Remember: You can change at any time and as many times as you like. You may even want to add golf to gardening as your Recreation. (I should warn you, however—golf is more difficult in Heaven than it was on Earth.) Ready to move on to Amendment Ten?"

Chapter 12

Heavenly Learning
(OR "You Not Only Learn, You Remember")

"Amendment Ten: Enjoy new learning for yourself, improve your communication with other Heavenly residents, and, especially, increase your ability to love others, including God and the Angels, as well as Earthlings like yourself. At times you may even think you're right up there with God. (Don't worry—you're not!)"

"How does learning new ideas, new facts and figures, and new interpretations from what we see, hear, and read in Heaven become more enjoyable in Heaven than on Earth?"

"Because learning will be easier, faster, and require less effort. You will make quicker connections with what you already know. God doesn't provide modern learning miracles, but He makes it easier for you to avoid distractions because a Heavenly Chorus of Harp Players provides white noise for all learning areas in Heaven. You'll notice the improvement over learning on Earth and be extremely pleased with God's system."

"Will I learn mostly with books or computers? Or from lecture/discussion led by the Newcomers who developed the courses that I take? Will I learn by doing, which I believe is the best way to learn?"

Eugene Jacobson

"At first, you'll use the method of learning that you liked best on Earth—reading. Soon, however, you'll be asking for help in learning how to use the computer to find what you're looking for. Plus, you'll learn new ways of storing the information that you find so you can get to it easily."

"You make it sound so easy. Are you sure?"

"Yup. To begin with, we're in Heaven, so much has been done to improve *how* we learn. And God's inventing new machines to help use the new methods to teach new ideas as quickly and easily as possible."

"So we can even work with Shakespeare in some of his plays? I know that learning by doing works well in both acting and directing classes. How can Newcomers learn in other ways in Shakespeare's works?"

"You can be an observer, noting actors' improvement in their vocal use, as well as physical movements—fighting, climbing, jumping, and moving as the character would. Lighting, set design and building, and music used in plays are wonderful methods of learning the pleasures of theatre as a technical team member. And when Shakespeare himself makes a suggestion during rehearsal, you really learn and remember what he has said."

"You mean that performances of Shakespeare's plays are given regularly in Heaven?"

"Regularly. Almost every day, in one part of Heaven or the other, at least one of his plays is being performed. And, thanks to God's plan to make all languages immediately understood by all Newcomers, regardless of the country where they lived or the language they spoke, all of Shakespeare's plays are in English and immediately understood by everyone in his native language."

"What is your reaction to the plays of Shakespeare in Heaven?"

"I have seen them all here at least once. Just as I did on Earth. My primary reaction is that I understand and enjoy every play in Heaven more than I did on Earth. One reason for the great performances is that each play is in rehearsal for a solid month. All day for about 12 hours, with some evenings as needed. (The usual Heavenly rule of ½ day for Work, ½ day for Recreation is sometimes suspended for this type of special project.) Yes, there are also other special projects in Heaven. For a limited time period God is especially flexible and understanding."

"How many performances are given for each Shakespeare play?"

"Shakespeare plays usually run for two weeks, including two matinees. But with the international interest in Shakespeare on Earth, you can imagine the waiting lists. At least a few weeks, maybe even longer. More modern popular plays, from not only the U.S. and Britain but also worldwide, usually run for one week, with only two weeks of rehearsals. Again, there is flexibility in rehearsal time if the play is long (Eugene O'Neill's *Long Day's Journey Into Night*, for instance.). God has another rule for Shakespeare plays—no audience member may see a second one until all of the people on the waiting lists have seen a play by the Bard. This works pretty well as less popular plays by this great English playwright are often chosen to avoid the long wait for a *Romeo and Juliet* or a *King Lear*. Probably more than you wanted to know?"

"That's my special interest—plays. But if someone else should read this, they might find it rather boring."

"So then, they can skip a few paragraphs, just skim through the material. Read like an adult should read."

"Ah, but some of us have a strict rule: I *always* read *all* of any book that I begin. I never skip, skim, or fail to finish a book."

"Then it's time to accept the greater Joys of Heaven. To begin with, *always* and *never* are ideas that are not often acceptable in Heaven. If a choice can be made (and in Heaven, those choices are always many), choose to be more flexible, put more ideas into the 'I can choose; I can be more flexible' category. Loosen up! Be more tolerant. Get more out of Heavenly Eternity."

"O.K. I'll try. But I'm not sure I can change that much."

"Oh, ye of little faith. Trust God. He'll help you to loosen up—even if you are Lutheran—and of Scandinavian background. And from Minnesota."

"I'm not sure any of those characteristics are very important in making my decisions, but I can change, I can become less hard-nosed, more flexible."

"Let's hope and pray so. Work at it."

"Sounds a bit like we're back to learning by doing again. I *will change* in order to fit into Heaven. A final comment on Shakespeare. His weaker plays like *Titus Andronicus*, with its rape, the victim's tongue and arms cut off so that she can't identify her attackers, etc., are still performed in Heaven? So that we can see how a creative person grows in the choice of plots, as well as the poetry of the dialogue, to remind ourselves that we can still get better in our lives, even as Newcomers in Heaven?"

"Absolutely. Hang on to that idea. And what was improved on Earth, both for you and for Shakespeare, can be improved beyond comparison when you do it in Heaven. Even subjects which you did not like or do well in, whether in high school or in college, may now not only interest you but also be a source of much learning and great joy."

"You keep using Earth terms for time—hours, days, years. Doesn't Heaven have its own terms for time?"

"You'll learn about Heaven's time when you're ready. Believe me, you're not ready yet."

"You mean I'm a slow learner? I'm dumb?"

"Now, now! Don't be defensive and get teacher-y on me. Just don't be in such a hurry to know everything at once! Try to have more patience. Learn gradually. For instance, how long do you think that you and I have been talking here in Heaven? In Earth time."

"That's tough. With no sunrise, no meals, no thirst (I never missed any meals on Earth). It can't be more than twelve hours."

"Nearly two weeks."

"Are you sure about the time?"

"I am. That's one of the things we're tested on before we're even considered for training as Heavenly Guides."

"Holy Smokes! Oops! Oh, that seemed to get by the Heavenly Language Censor. How come?"

"Because Holy Smokes is pretty mild. And you haven't been in Heaven very long yet. Mild oaths and slang will soon disappear from your speech and writing. Those words are only used in Heaven for humor. Three or four times a year, Mark Twain teaches a class, usually about 1,000 Newcomers in each session, on how to use humor with large audiences, reading selections from his own works. He also teaches a smaller class of 25 about humor in writing. With less interest in writing, Twain just waits until the class hits the size limit and then teaches a 3-week course, Humor in Writing. Another learning by doing class."

"So learning in Heaven is a no-problem system?"

"There's at least one problem that God is still working on: The Waiting Lists. Waits due to a filled class or workshop cause minor irritations, but they're soon forgotten, even by those who were Republicans on Earth. Eternity puts a different slant on *do it now*. Those in need of more humor in their Heavenly lives often include Lutherans. They make up about 10% of every Mark Twain class. At least they know their Earthly weaknesses and are willing to use humor to solve their Heavenly problems. Lutherans from the Missouri and Wisconsin Synods seem to need all the help that God can give them. Being so conservative in most of what they do and how they talk about themselves, they need help to lighten up, even in Heaven."

"Let's leave the Lutherans alone for awhile, O.K.?"

"Sure. Sorry. They're such easy targets. But this is Heaven. I'd better act more kind and loving. After all, Lutherans are not much different from other conservative religious groups. Some different, but not a lot!"

"Onward and upward?"

"Yup. I want to repeat that you may quit whatever you are studying, whether for your Eternal Life Work or Eternal Recreation, at any time, without fear of criticism or negative evaluation. God knows that you learn by your mistakes. So if you get bored, change your mind about what you're interested in, find the subject too complex (seldom a problem, but even in Heaven we make mistakes), give it up! Quit! Start over on something new. Accept God's forgiveness and love. Sorry—I tend to overdo that bit in my Guiding. I promise not to repeat that comment for at least a couple of days!"

"Good! I'll remind you if necessary. I'm thinking I'd like to try a foreign language or two for the Recreation side of the ledger in Heaven. I've studied Latin (in high school and college), plus German and Norwegian. The same problem came up in each language that I studied. I got along well enough with the grammar of all my languages (although I don't recall using the Latin Ablative Case very often after the class was over), but the vocabulary was very hard for me to keep up with. I couldn't memorize the all new words and idioms that were added to our vocabularies in every lesson. I never did at all well without a dictionary in any foreign language. Any chance I'd learn quicker and better in Heaven? I'm really in love with the look of Chinese and Japanese languages, for instance. Not just words spelled with letters from an alphabet, but picture languages, somewhat like the hieroglyphics of the Egyptians."

"Of course you will! Much like the immersion method used on Earth, where you live with other people who may already know the language, or, like you, are studying the language for the first time. There's a little sign language going on at first, but everyone soon uses the language *all* the time! However, Heaven goes even further. Not only do you speak only the language you're studying, but you live in an area like the original geography on Earth (in the mountains or on a seashore), plus you wear the native clothing, eat the native food, and learn the habits of the people you're studying."

"Does God allow you to cheat if you really get stuck? Do the foreign words get translated into English if I don't understand something?"

"It's a little more complicated than that. God has suspended the automatic translation, which is normally used in Heaven. Instead, no automatic translation takes place in a Learning a Language Class, but the super-helpful Angel Assistants are allowed to help you by translating any word, phrase, or sentence that has you stumped. In fact, in the first sessions there's a one-on-one ratio of Helpful Angels for the new students. As the class ability increases, fewer Angels are needed for the new students. A final ratio of about 1 to 6 is used, even at the end of the class."

"How long do these classes last—a few weeks, a month, a year?"

"It depends on the difficulty of the language and the learning skills of the students. By the way, the Heavenly Language Teachers found out that their students seemed to learn faster when they were in class or studied for 12 hours, and then went to 12 hours of recreation, which was usually not tied in with the language being studied. There are almost always exceptions to the rules and God said, 'If it works, do it! Stick to the regular 12/12 schedule when it helps in studying a foreign language."

"I'm a little surprised at how flexible God is. Almost as if rules are made to be broken."

"You're close! The 'Do no physical or psychological harm to your Neighbor on Earth and in Heaven' is one that is an absolute. No exceptions that I've ever heard of."

"If you're going to be a stickler on rules and laws, that's a great place to begin. I think I'm ready to start my classes for both Work and Recreation."

"Are you sure?"

"Yes. Can't we start now?"

"Actually, we can. You may take a Work Study course and a Recreation Study course with approximately 50/50 time on each course."

"And all the Newcomers in the classes have changed in Heaven so that they no longer need to eat or sleep?"

"If some Newcomer should need to eat and sleep, he will be allowed a snack and a brief nap. What two courses do you want? Plus, I'll need a little more information from you."

"I want to be a teacher of English (American), but I don't know which special subject I would teach. And I'd like to teach my courses using English."

"No problem. Your advanced courses in English and American Literature will help you decide on which additional courses you will train for and then teach. Nearly all courses teach by doing. You'll be helping a fellow student or someone outside of the class in a one-to-one pairing. Do you think you'd have any trouble learning and teaching at the same time, as I've described the classes?"

"None. Sounds great! These new methods of learning were developed here in Heaven?"

"Right. And your class for Recreation?'

"Some type of Chinese, preferably not Mandarin. Filling in with something more physical—gardening (which I already chose), golf, or fishing. Is fishing allowed in Heaven?"

"Yes, fishing is allowed. But you may not use barbed hooks. Plus, all fish are catch and release. The fish are very cooperative, however. They allow you to measure and weigh them before they jump back in the water. You'll have a variety of possible species of fish to catch— bass, sunfish, northerns, etc."

"How many fish can you catch each day? How big are they?"

"No limit—fish until you are tired. Most fish weigh from one pound to ten pounds, with one fish in each lake weighing 25 pounds. And Heaven has hundreds of rivers, ponds, and lakes where you can fish."

"Even the fishing sounds Heavenly. Do we have other things to do before my classes begin?"

"We need to review briefly the 10 Amendments and your reaction to each of them. Then I will ask if you want to go alone to your classes or if you want me to stay with you while you get started."

"Let's do the 10 Amendments Review first. After that, I'd like a little time to decide about your continuing to be my Guide."

Chapter 13

The 10 Amendments Revisited
(OR "Did You Change Your Mind?")

"After we review the 10 Amendments, I will ask you how my work as a Guide could be improved."

"I'll do my best to make some suggestions. After all, I am a teacher—and that's what teachers do."

Grinning, Roger replied, "I was afraid of that. O.K. Let's do the review. 'Amendment One – You feel great joy because you are in Heaven. (And it only gets better.)' "

"That's true. I could hardly believe I was in Heaven at first. God's Grace was enough even for *me* to get to Heaven. I'm even lighter on my feet."

"You're walking on Heavenly air. That's a fairly common thing for Newcomers, especially those whose faith is rather vague and misty. When Mother Teresa got to Heaven, her feet were solidly on the ground—it was as she had always imagined it. Although she was a little surprised at the welcoming fanfare. And she was visibly shocked when the Father, Son, and Holy Spirit stepped forward to greet her. Before They could stop her, she threw herself at Their feet. They helped her up at once and dusted her off carefully (although there's no dust in Heaven!). But everyone watching (Newcomers, Angels, and other Staff

Members) understood the symbolism of Their action. Mother Teresa got over her awe fairly quickly and began to chat with the Holy Three. God has prepared a special Heaven for every Newcomer, which means there are a lot of different Heavens for everyone from Earth. Are you ready for Amendment Two?"

"Yup. Let's do it!"

"Amendment Two – When you arrive in Heaven, your body will be the age and weight you were when you died. You may experiment with any body changes that you wish to make. (Ask your Guide for complete instructions.) You look a little younger than when you first arrived. Are you satisfied with how you look?"

"Pretty close. I'd like to end up to be in my mid-40's and weigh the 150 pounds that I did when I got out of the Army in 1953. Is it true, that regardless of how I change, anyone who knew me on Earth will see me at the age and weight that they remember?"

"Yes, anyone who saw you on Earth will remember their strongest impression of you there. In their minds, God will change the present image they receive of you to how they remember you best."

"Some of God's special methods seem a little complicated to me."

"The main reason that God sets up this special process is so that a person's family and friends will immediately recognize everyone they knew on earth when seeing them in Heaven. Later, they may see that person as he really is in H eaven today. O.K.?"

"I guess so. I need to think about it a little more."

"You accept the main idea, so this Amendment is no problem for your acceptance into Heaven. Ready for Amendment Three?"

"Shoot!"

"Amendment Three – At first, what you see and hear in Heaven will be what you expected Heaven to be. (This Heaven will change.)"

"As you recall, I couldn't really see you and St. Peter clearly when I first woke up in Heaven."

"Because you weren't sure what Heaven looked like—or even if it existed. And, if Heaven existed, whether you'd get in. You couldn't imagine God's limitless Grace."

One Man's Heaven

"When you came over to talk to me, you became clearer. I began to believe in Heaven. By the way, what was it that you were arguing about with St. Peter?"

"I wouldn't exactly call it arguing. A simple Guide like me is in no position to argue with any of the Big Shots of Heaven. I simply pointed out that for the last several months (night and day), I had been the guide for a pastor. Yup, a genuine Missouri Synod minister. He still needed to eat and to sleep during every 24 hours. But he didn't eat enough or sleep enough to give me much rest from his questions about Heaven and objections to the 10 Amendments. By the end of six months, he ate and slept less, but he talked more and more. I've never had anyone else take over my work as a Guide to a Newcomer, but with this guy I came close!"

"Was he cranky, hard to deal with, difficult to convince?"

"No, but he did one thing that almost drove me crazy. He had a small, palm-sized notebook in his hand when he arrived in Heaven. Before he died, he requested that the notebook should be slipped under his hands, folded around the cross on his chest, in the casket. So the cross and the notebook both got to Heaven with him. His plan worked—I don't know how!"

"And the trouble was...?"

"Although he lost the cross the first day, he used the notebook constantly. I tried over and over to convince him that everything that we said to each other would be burned into his memory forever. But, no, he wasn't convinced, even when it worked perfectly when we checked it out. Instead, he had to write down every word of every question and every answer. Using the exact words each time! Do you have any idea about how much time this takes—even in Eternity?"

I couldn't help myself. I started laughing and couldn't quit!

"Now stop that! I don't mind your laughing a bit at my expense, but when you fall down on the ground and can't breathe, that's too much. Now, get up! Stop it!"

I tried. I really did. I had laughed almost this hard just once on Earth, but this was twice as much fun! It seems that even laughter is better in Heaven. I was having a little trouble breathing, gasping for air. But I had no pain, no concern about anything. But I couldn't stop laughing, couldn't get myself up off the ground. It was one of the best experiences I've ever had. Roger gave up on me fairly soon and walked away. I caught him checking on me every few minutes. To be sure that I didn't...what? Die? Not likely—I'm already in Heaven. I asked Roger later if anything like my uncontrolled laughter had ever happened to him before as a Heavenly Guide. He not only said, "no," but his tone of voice told me that it would never happen to him again. At last, I got control of myself—after a violent half hour. I struggled to my feet, coughed a couple of times, then walked slowly over to Roger.

"I'm sorry—I didn't mean to laugh at—"

Roger held up his right hand for silence, then spoke.

"You don't need to apologize. I spent the last fifteen minutes chuckling at my own experience with this pastor. I have several pictures in my mind which show how ridiculous we looked as we scowled and jabbered at one another. And this went on for months! I was supposed to be in charge. If something went wrong, it was my job to make it right. Perhaps the Guide Teaching Faculty will have suggestions for solving the problem of time-consuming note-taking."

"Are there any other problems with being Guides for Newcomers?"

"One outstanding problem: Most of the Newcomers speak in short sentences. But a few of them, especially teachers, preachers, and U.S. Senators know that 'The Devil is in the details,' and the Senators in particular love the details!"

"I'm curious. How long did you say that you worked with that Lutheran pastor?"

Roger sighed. "Nearly 18 months. His Guide told us that even Einstein took only a year, and Einstein asked good questions."

"How long does it look like I'll take?"

"A couple more weeks—at the most! You're not too bad for a college professor. At least you encourage me to talk more than you do."

"Didn't the Pastor—?"

"No, he didn't. I only got to talk about 10% of the time. I hate to think of the length of his sermons! That's enough. Going on?"

I nodded.

"Amendment Four: Not long after you get to Heaven, you will choose whether you wish to remain in Heaven, return to Earth, or go to Hell. (You may visit Hell at any time, returning to Heaven whenever you want. Few people remain in Hell very long.)"

"There's no question in my mind. I'd like to stay in Heaven."

"No big surprise there. Over 90% of Newcomers choose Heaven immediately."

"And the other 10% are mostly Hindus and Buddhists?" I asked. "They have it firmly in their minds that they must keep returning to Earth, getting to be better people each time, until they reach Nirvana (the perfection of no longer being an individual but a part of God)."

"That's right," Roger said. "Nearly all of the Asian religious folks find it difficult to accept the idea of God's complete forgiveness for sins and the gift of Heaven for Eternity. But with the help of the Guides and some time to let the ideas of Universal Salvation surround them, 90% of these Return-to-Earth Newcomers choose Heaven."

"And those who choose Hell, usually as a matter of Free Will, are usually back in Heaven in a week or two? But don't the Return-to-Earth folks have to wait longer than the others before they get another chance to choose Heaven because they have to die again while on Earth? So less than 1% of all the Newcomers end up returning to Earth?'

"That is correct. By the way, you seem to be thinking about Angels during our present discussion. Any reason why?"

"I see and hear more of the Heavenly Harp Angels than I did earlier. What changed?"

"You did. When you first got to Heaven, your belief in Angels was pretty weak and vague. But after you saw a few of them, you believed more in Angels, so you saw and heard more of them. You even noticed that most Angels have Silver Tongues to contrast with their Golden Harps."

"Were there Angels near me when I was on Earth, too?"

"Not very many. More Angels would be seen if folks on Earth would believe in them more strongly. The people on Earth who see Angels quite regularly are innocent young children, hard-working Mother Teresas, and devout Joans of Arc. Very few men on Earth will see Angels, even in their dreams."

In my life on Earth, I don't remember ever discussing Angels with either male or female friends. For a man to talk about Angels wasn't masculine."

"That's part of what Heaven is all about. You change the wrong ideas you had about Heaven, God, even your fellow human beings."

"Heaven, Hell, or Earth again. For me—Heaven! And on to the next Amendment?"

"Amendment Five – There is no sex in Heaven (either in thought or action). God tried permitting the Cave People to have sex, but it was just too noisy and created too many problems. God's decision for NO SEX has been final for centuries and is not apt to be changed."

"Maybe it's just that I'm almost 80 years old, but I see no problem for me on this rule. What about others, some of whom have been promised a staggering number of virgins if they sacrifice their lives for a religious cause?"

"God has all that taken care of. If you have no thoughts about sex once you're in Heaven it's no longer a problem."

"O.K. What about the husbands/wives/lovers who can't wait to be reunited with a loved one in Heaven? Sex is usually not discussed in 'I can't wait to be reunited with...,' but the suggestion is there."

"No problem: no sex. The Joys of Heaven will more than make up for the loss of sex."

"In the minds of even the most God-loving Earthlings (perhaps more men than women), their thought is 'sex is really great on Earth. If everything's supposed to be better in Heaven, how great would sex be?'"

"Still no problem. If you don't think about sex, the problem is solved before it begins. You'll never worry about sex in Heaven—it's an Earth thing."

"Why was I allowed to talk about sex just now when no one is allowed sexual thoughts or actions?"

"Because you (and all other Newcomers) are allowed to ask any questions when the 10 Amendments are covered with a Heavenly Guide. But that's it—after the Fifth Amendment discussion, Newcomers won't even recall what was said. Sex is gone, out, kaput!"

"O.K. No problem, no further discussion about...?" And I lost my train of thought.

"Aha! It's working! On to Amendment Six – You may visit the members of your family who got to Heaven before you did. (Special permission is required if you visit them in Hell.) Do not expect too much of your first visit. Especially if you are Lutherans. You will recognize one another easily, probably kiss and embrace (unless you are of Scandinavian descent). You will probably find that your family members have already made a smooth transition to Heaven and will feel much closer to God than to you."

"I'm really looking forward to seeing my Mom and Dad, plus my maternal Grandmother, whom I lived with off and on in town, when I had High School play rehearsals after school. Could I see them fairly soon?"

"Right after we finish this final review of the 10 Amendments."

"Good! Will other family members be there?"

"Only if you think of them and want them"

"And friends? I have about half a dozen special friends whom I would like to see and talk to."

"No problem. We'll schedule them for later."

"But unlike many of our too-close relationships with our families on Earth, God will still be Number One."

"Yes, indeed. Now for Amendment Seven – You will quickly learn that whatever you do in Heaven is a means of worshipping God—and serving your fellow Newcomers. No special churches or altars or rituals are used. But, yes, there are helpful Angels—most of them with harps—who will assist you if you have any questions or need advice about proper methods of worship."

"Just a brief question on Angels: Do they always have harps?"

"No, not always. Because of their assistance in teaching of all kinds, Angels are next to God in the Joy they create in Heaven among the Newcomers."

"The Angels are really good at their jobs?"

"Super! And they keep getting better all the time. What the Angels have always been known for are their smiles. Big broad, friendly grins which make everyone (including the Big Three) feel happier, better about themselves, and truly feel the Joy of Heaven."

"So, all I have to do is to start working."

"Right. But you need to remind yourself that work includes learning. And that, even as you're learning, you need to spend 12 hours a day in Recreation."

"I understand that Work and Recreation in Heaven are ways of worshipping God, but I'm a little confused about how this serves Newcomers in Heaven."

"I don't know the complete answer to that question. But God feels that Newcomers in Heaven who improve the quality of their lives are also able to express their love of God and other Newcomers more strongly. Does that help?"

"I need more time to think about that."

"No problem. Whether you believe it or not, the Worship and Serve Plan continues to make Heaven even better. Any other comments?"

"I just need a little time, O.K.?"

"Sure. Time is no problem. May we go on?"

"Yes! Bring on Amendment Eight!"

Amendment Eight – All people go to Heaven when they die (Universal Salvation). This idea is not accepted by all Newcomers when they first enter Heaven. We need to remember God makes the rules here. With all the varying Earthly ideas about Heaven which the Newcomers bring with them, at first there are many Heavens. God allows all Newcomers to find Heaven as they imagined It. Gradually, they learn to accept God's Heaven. And the Real Thing is much better!"

"That's a little confusing. Do you mean that the Heaven that I am in is the result of what I thought Heaven would be?"

"Yes. And already you've made some changes in your ideas about Heaven. Do you remember your negative attitude toward Angels? How many did you see at first? How many Harps did you hear?"

"I saw few Angels, heard no Harps. Now I see busy Angels all around me, with harp music becoming louder and more soothing all the time. Are there any other unexpected differences in Heaven that some Newcomers find difficult to accept?"

"As you expect, some Newcomers are even shocked to find other religions, other races, even unbelievers among fellow Newcomers. God has this figured out, too—just as He gives all Newcomers time to get used to Heaven as it is, starting with what they expected, so He is kind to everyone, giving them time to change. A few hard-headed folks get impatient with Heaven and choose to visit Hell, even a couple times. But they always return to Heaven and change gradually. And Heaven keeps getting better and better, the longer we're here."

"How come I never read that in the Bible? Nor did I ever hear it from a member of the clergy."

"They probably never considered this possibility, and God chose not to tell them. I don't know why. But in Heaven we just keep getting better and better. Didn't you have a similar statement that you kept repeating when you were first married, until you almost drove your wife crazy? Anyway, she begged you to stop–and surprising everyone, including yourself, you stopped. Exactly what did you say?"

"It was awful! Neither true nor clever, just annoying. I'm too embarrassed to say it again."

"Go ahead. In Heaven, this will be treated like one of your bad jokes—once you say it, neither you nor anyone else in Heaven will ever be able to repeat it again."

"O.K." I sighed. "I said, 'Every day, in every way, I'm getting better and better!' "

"Even if you were kidding (I know you were!), the superior attitude, the lack of wit or humor in your remark—"

"Thank God I'm in Heaven! I don't think that I could take any more of this criticism on Earth."

"Do you think I just now overdid it?"

Grinning, I replied, "Of course not. I feel no bitterness, no desire to hurt, from you. Just giving me a bad time! (Well-deserved!) And on we go? 'All Newcomers will find that Heaven isn't what they expected—it's better!' "

"Eternity is a good place for leaving the Old behind and accepting the New!"

"God has created Perfection for Eternity. What more could we ask? On to the next Amendment!"

"Amendment Nine – Feel free to try as many Heavenly Experiences and Activities as you like. Your Goal is to decide how you will worship God and serve your Neighbors in Heaven—for Eternity! No rush: you may make changes in your plans at any time, with no limit on the number of changes that you make. With Eternity, you have plenty of time."

"Haven't I pretty well decided on what I'll do, at least to begin with? Learning to teach better, for half of each day as Work and the other half as some kind of Chinese for my Recreation? By the way, how long do we keep using Earth Time here in Heaven?"

"Until Earth Time is no longer a part of your thinking. You'll notice that I'm still using the word *decade* after years in Heaven."

"I can drop a class or change it if I'm not doing well, or if I don't like what I'm learning. No questions asked?"

"None. But it's unlikely that you will do poorly or dislike any class. The instructors are top-notch in their fields, all of them like students, and numerous assistants (usually Angels) for every class mean a lot of one-on-one learning."

"How does God keep track of how many instructors are needed? With millions of new Newcomers each year, and especially now from the big Asian countries, like China, how does God know what subjects and how many instructors will be needed?"

"God has a lot of help. And computers make the planning and actual classes easier to schedule. Computer programmers and operators keep information up-to-date and moving. Besides—"

"I know, I know! This is Heaven, and not only are all things possible, they are done! Another question: How many classes may a Newcomer take at one time?"

"Most Newcomers take at least two courses at a time--usually one for Work and the other for Recreation. Many people take up to six courses during the same time, both for the sake of variety and because it's possible with 24 hours available each day and for the six days a week for Work/Recreation."

"How is that possible?"

"We haven't talked about this much up to now, but you've experienced two major changes here in Heaven. During the nearly three weeks you've been here, you have scarcely eaten and briefly slept."

"Is this unusual?"

"Not terribly. About 90% of all Newcomers adapt gradually to no eating and no sleeping. The Newcomers who spent most of their lives on Earth being hungry have enough to eat in Heaven for the first time. Sometimes they eat heartily for a week or even a month. Surprisingly, many of these hungry people take only a week to ten days to change to the No Eating Required Rule of Heaven. God could simply change all Newcomers' need to eat or sleep. But He prefers to let Newcomers make these changes more gradually by themselves."

"I don't remember sleeping at all since I got here. Did I?"

"Yup—sort of super catnaps, usually for less than ten seconds each time. But you had a total of 596 catnaps, according to my computer, which counts everything you do and say."

"I don't remember even one time when I fell asleep!"

"Because you *were* asleep! With your eyes closed and not talking (God rewards us with minor miracles)."

"Hmmm. And my eating? Did I?"

"Sort of—four times in the last three weeks. You had just a small sip of Heavenly Nectar each time. You felt thirsty, a nearby Angel got your message and swooped down to hold a silver goblet to your lips. In fact, you took a good gulp each time. Were you a Methodist on your way to becoming a Lutheran?"

"When I was quite young, I attended a Methodist Sunday School. Later, I was confirmed in the Lutheran Church. Why?"

"Methodists serve grape juice for their communion. They tend to gulp. If they become Lutheran, they sometimes still gulp. After a choke or two, they learn to sip."

"That's not something I have to believe in order to stay in Heaven, is it?"

"No, it's just based on my observations while on Earth. I could be wrong."

"I'm glad to hear that—someone who admits he might be wrong. In Heaven, not on Earth."

"Are you done?"

I grinned.

"O.K., back to eating and sleeping in Heaven. God has set up a process where all food is digested in the body, but the end product is a Heavenly Perfume that is barely noticed in the Heavenly Air. Have you noticed this perfume at all?"

"Barely. Not at all when I first got to Heaven. Later, a faint whiff now and then. It was very delicate, reminding me of lilacs on Earth. But a very faint, almost mysterious odor. Nice."

"Gradually, you'll smell a hint of frankincense in the air. As it gets stronger, it will help you to worship God, reminding you of the Bible stories you heard as a child. For the unbeliever, the original smell is coffee, slowly switching to the individual unbeliever's favorite fragrance on Earth. Such as Chanel #5."

"My whole idea about Heaven has been enlarged by everything you've told me. I'm almost overwhelmed—but still eager to learn more!"

"And you will learn more. With your own eyes, ears, even your nose, you will develop a greater understanding and appreciation of Heaven."

"Hallelujah! Oops! That's not very Lutheran."

"No, but it's very Heavenly."

"If we're going to finish our review of the 10 Amendments, do we need to move on?"

"You're helping me with my job—keep moving ahead. Amendment Ten – Enjoy new learning for yourself, improve your communication with other Heavenly residents, and, especially, increase your ability to love others. Including God and the Angels, as well as Earthling like yourself. At times you may even think you're right there with God (don't worry – you're not!)."

"We've agreed on my Work and Recreation Class schedule. But how will what I learn help me to love God and others?"

"You will practice new methods of communication. You will learn what others want you to do for them just by looking at them and focusing on what they say. Some of these folks will become your close friends. Most of all, you will have an unlimited variety of Training, Working, and Recreational activities during which you will meet people from other countries, other cultures, with other Earthly beliefs (or unbeliefs) about God and Heaven. You will learn a lot from your classes, but you will also be reminded of a basic skill from Earth: listening. And you'll get better at it. You'll let others talk more than you do. As your Pastor, Dr. Joel Flugstad, once said, 'Whatever promotes life in the other is Love.' Being a sincere, attentive listener is certainly an act of Love."

"I never get quite the answers that I expect from you, Roger."

"Is that good?"

"Very! You make me think in a different direction from the one I have in mind."

"Do I ever confuse you? I don't try to do that, you know."

"Occasionally, you startle. But usually I clearly understand what you say."

"Give me an example, please."

"I've been a little afraid after something you said. You told me that as Angels cruise above our Earthlings in Heaven, they can sense that we need something. I was feeling a little thirsty, and suddenly an Angel with a silver chalice was offering me Heavenly Punch."

"What's wrong with that?"

"A couple of things. When that Angel appeared next to me, without a sound, it almost scared the Hallelujah out of me. Those babies are big—and burly! And this one was female!"

"Not to worry. The Angels are all the same size, about 6'2" but with their flying around, sometimes at supersonic speeds, they're in very good shape—pretty muscular. Does that bother you?"

"I'm just not used to hulking Angels right next to me. Because of a few vague Biblical verses, I imagined the Angels were smaller, usually playing a harp, and definitely not muscular."

"On this subject, the trouble is not with Heaven or the Angels, but you. You need to get with it. Forget your Earthly prejudices about Angels."

"Just warn me so I can brace myself for the sudden whirring of wings, followed by the overpowering body of an Angel."

"Some of the little old ladies up here have a sign on their heads: Leave me alone until I call for help. Angels honor these signs and no longer trip over little ladies in their rush to provide airplanes for them. Actually, many of the ladies still appreciate strong male bodies next to them, even if God has cut off sexual thoughts and reactions. These husky Angels make Heaven more joyful for quite a few older Newcomers."

"If you say so. As long as the Angels don't scare the bejabbers out of me. I'll tell you when I'll be up to having them hovering over my head again."

"O.K. Any final words about Amendment Ten?"

"I guess not. All I have to do is work hard, play hard, and worship God with all I say and do. Plus serve and love my fellow Earthlings in Heaven. All easy—with the help of God."

"You got it! So, you've pretty well accepted the 10 Heavenly Amendments and are firmly housed in Heaven, in the bosom of God."

"O.K., but that bosom of God part is a little overboard for a stiff-necked Scandinavian from Minnesota."

"Maybe you'll loosen up a bit in Heaven. God would like you to do that."

"And what God wants, He gets. Are we ready for…?"

"Yes, we're ready for the Wrap-up. The Last Lap!"

Chapter 14:

The Wrap-up
(OR "Though God is for Eternity, He Encourages
Endings, When They are Appropriate")

"I told you that I wanted your suggestions about how I could improve myself as a Heavenly Guide."
"Yes, you did. And I can hardly wait!"
"You're a little too eager. I'd like to make a few suggestions to you before you begin. O.K.?"
"I'm ready. Shoot!"
"Some of your Earthly word choices seem out of place here in Heaven. 'Shoot!' just makes me think of the National Rifle Association. Were you a member of that organization on Earth?"
"No, although I hunted pheasants and ducks with my 20-gauge from the time I was a boy until I was in my thirties in Colorado. But when we moved to Pennsylvania and Florida for my teaching jobs, bird-hunting areas were just too hard to get to. I never joined the American Legion either, although I spent two years during the Korean War in the Army (in the State-side Southern Zone—South Carolina and Georgia). I wasn't much of a joiner, and we didn't even become regular Lutheran church-goers until our two sons, Tom and Andrew, were born."

"That was when you and your wife began attending Adult Sunday School Classes in the Lutheran Church? So you developed some additional understanding of Christianity and some idea of what God was like?"

"Yes, but we began to hear and read that there were many ways to look for God. Current social issues caused us some problems too, in our local congregations. I remember sitting in an Adult Sunday School Class (around a table in the church kitchen) in Bethlehem, PA. Our discussion had strayed from the usual Bible study to the rights of blacks in the U.S. during the unsettled 1960s. I made the moderate statement, perhaps not in a moderate tone (I don't remember how heated the discussion had been), that after 100 years perhaps it was about time that blacks had equal rights at work, in selecting any area for purchasing a home, and for other legal rights. A nice, 30ish father, normally smiling and friendly, stood up, leaned across the table and shook his finger at me as he shouted, 'You're nothing but a [ ] liberal!' Then he sat down, angrily. I slid back in my chair, as much surprised by his use of 'liberal' as a negative word as by his heated reaction. Being Lutheran, we soon settled down, but this discussion of civil rights had ended, at least for that Sunday. Later, in Florida but more so in Oklahoma certain words such as 'union,' 'liberal,' and 'gay' were better left out of Adult Sunday School discussions."

"You don't think that your self-righteous attitude (I'm guessing here) about this subject may have been at least part of the problem in the discussion? Why were you so surprised when this happened to you? Because you're really such a good guy, well-meaning, not getting too loud (permit me a mild ho ho ho, here, please), sounding like 'I'm always right' in your tone of voice?"

"Pardon me for not being more upset by your 'always right' comment. I've heard it before, but, coming from you, it stops me short. I'll work on that here in Heaven."

"You don't have to work too hard. God has already toned you down a little for Heaven. You may have noticed that you don't get as upset about criticism as you did on Earth."

"What about my temper?"

"Gone!"

"My cute, cutting remarks?"

"Gone at last! Gone at last! Thank God Almighty—gone at last!"

"But isn't Heaven going to be kind of dull?"

"Never! God has more surprises for you (and all other Newcomers) than you, being human and limited, can imagine."

"Gotcha. Any more questions?"

"Yes, but try for short answers this time. You're still too long-winded—you sound like a professor or a politician. Do you think you'll get this book we're talking our way through published? You don't say much that's new or particularly entertaining."

"I don't know. Maybe God will help me find a way."

"And what do you hope to accomplish with this little book?"

"I hope that what I write about my fictitious Heaven will cause some readers to think about a couple of the ideas (not my own—as you notice, I borrow often) that I've included. Such important ideas as Universal Salvation, God's limitless Grace, and our own vagueness in imagining what Heaven is like. Maybe each of us will have our own Heaven, just as we imagine it. As Lutherans, we've been taught that we get to Heaven only by the Grace of God. If God wants us, and we believe He does, He will bring us to Heaven. Our Free Will is no match for the power of God. Could I be wrong? Saints preserve us—of course! Shouldn't we be encouraged to pray for the best, knowing that God wants the best for us?"

"And that's the short answer?"

"No, but I'm going to keep my eyes open. I feel that I'm going to see stuff that no Newcomer has ever seen before."

"Why not have an Angel help you find your answers?"

"I'll do that. Now, you wanted me to tell you how I thought you could improve as a Heavenly Guide, right? I'll let you respond after each of my comments."

"You have a list?"

"You betcha!"

"Where is it?"

"In my head."

"A dangerous place."

"May I begin?"

Roger nodded, perhaps a bit nervously. "As a prime example myself, couldn't you get more Guiding done if you didn't allow the Newcomer such long answers and comments?"

"We were taught, very carefully, to let each Newcomer talk as much as that person wanted to. You're pretty talky, but you're not the worst kind. The scary ones are those who hardly talked at all on Earth. Once they get to Heaven and feel safe here, they go on and on. We do have a method of making responses shorter. We ask them to write out their answers if they talk too long. Usually, after one long answer written out—or the most, two—they get the message."

"Are there any other problems?"

"Well, the primary rule that any favorite stories that are told in Heaven may never be repeated here made for a peculiar exception. Some Old-timers wanted to tell a story or two so much that they took a short trip to Hell to escape the rule and tell the forbidden story again. (The no-repeat rule applies only in Heaven.) God thinks that use of Hell is rather funny. Particularly as the stories send some Hell visitors back to Heaven more quickly."

"What about asking a Newcomer to talk more about his life on Earth, particularly problems? As a sort of verbal catharsis, a cleaning out/getting rid of some old hang-ups by talking about them. You didn't ask me very much at all."

"In your case, no major problems on Earth showed up in our files. You still have some concerns about wishing that you had taught better by doing things differently (more learning by doing, listening to what students suggested, etc.). Most good teachers have some areas where they could have improved. But you have learned to accept what you did in the past. Also, you'll probably be able to apply new solutions to some of your problems in your continued teaching in Heaven."

"You guys really seem to know what you're doing. Did you happen to pick up any new ideas while you were guiding me?"

One Man's Heaven

"Some. You could have made a greater number of positive comments as we went along, but I realize that you're both Scandinavian and a Lutheran, so I didn't expect too much."

My face showed shock at this remark.

"Easy, easy. That's a little bit of my Heavenly humor. Obviously, I'm not a very good jokester. We're encouraged not to use much humor. Somehow, Guides' humor tends to fall flat. Or shake the Newcomer up. Sorry—I'm still learning, too!"

"I saw some of my humor in your criticism. I'll try to be more careful in the future. At least quite a few of my tired old stories are gone!"

"Any further suggestions?"

"No, you seem to have it all under control. I was impressed: you let me talk freely, but you still answered all my questions. Oh, wait—I do have a final question: why are you named Roger? My best friend in high school was called Roger. But you're not the Roger I knew. He died more than eight years ago. His younger brother, Father Richard, who presided over Roger's funeral, said that Roger had gone ahead to Heaven to make a place for him. But is there a special reason why you have Roger's name as my Guide?"

"Yes, there is. God wanted you to have something to remind you of Earth but also welcome you to Heaven. My name, on Earth in England, was Roger."

"Roger's name did help me feel more at home. So the real Roger wouldn't have worked as my Guide?"

"Roger is very busy. He thinks more about his Work here in Heaven now than about his past life on Earth. Roger spends most of his time making wooden toys for kids in Heaven, just as he made them for his own grandchildren on Earth. He said that he looks forward to seeing you again, but he understands (as you do) that relationships with friends and even with family members may not be as strong as they were on Earth. Roger has many new friends in Heaven, is liked by everyone he meets, and keeps his calm, even-tempered behavior in Heaven. Even better than when he was on Earth. He says he is looking forward to being reunited with his wife, Mildred and his children."

"I understand Roger being busy in Heaven; he was always busy on Earth, too. I look forward to meeting him one day soon."

"And you still hope to publish a copy of this conversation that we've had?"

"Yes, with God's help. These ideas are fiction, but I believe God encourages us to think, to question, even the existence of Himself and Heaven. This is my idea of what I'd like my Heaven to be. I'm not at all certain that what I would like will be there. Actually, I'm pretty sure it will be better. I believe that many of us need to think more about Heaven. Maybe God will even have special Heavens for each of us—at least at first. Perhaps we can even have a taste of Heaven here on Earth if we work on it. One of our Lutheran pastors said, 'Heaven is now,' meaning that we should begin to know the joy of Heaven while still on Earth. Worshipping God and helping our Neighbors (all people on Earth) as our religion says we should."

"Do you feel that writing down your thoughts has helped you to believe more strongly, more definitely in God and Heaven?"

"Yes. And my use of humor in kidding Scandinavians, particularly Lutherans, plus teachers/professors was made acceptable, I hope, by my being all of those myself. If I offended anyone, I apologize. If I caused anyone to do a little thinking, especially about God and Heaven, but also how we're to use our lives on Earth to worship God and serve our neighbors, I'm satisfied." I hesitated. "So now we part?"

"For the time being. After talking together, we'll never be quite the same. We have come to know one another. May our Eternity in Heaven be even more joyous than what we hope for. I'm sure: 'it will be so' because of God's love and boundless Grace!"

"Amen. Amen. Amen."

Printed in the United States
80559LV00002B/307-333